In the news they've been talking about how likely it is for a black male teenager to get shot and killed—especially in my neighborhood. They say it's even more likely that in a couple of years I'll be carrying a gun.

But what they don't know is what a difference God's made in my life. Ever since I was three I've been going to Sunday school, and I've learned about God and His ways. And I made up my mind to follow Jesus.

No, you'll never see me with a gun shooting anyone. Ever! Because no matter what's going on around me, I am standing for Jesus.

Vincent
age 12

When I go to Sunday school, I feel good to be there. It is so much fun with the games we play, and the best thing is when we talk about God. Every Saturday I get up in the morning thinking that at 3 P.M. I have to be ready to go. Then I go and come back home and tell my parents all about it.

Hernan
age 11

I like Sunday school. I like to go to God's house and hear what is right and what is wrong, and I like the games. I like to joke around, but not in God's house. I won't play around.

Edwin
age 10

Dear Bill, I love Sunday school, and I like the games, and I love the people in there, and the thing I love most about Sunday school is the preaching. I just love your preaching.

Nigeria
age 8

I love Sunday school for a couple of reasons:

1) They teach me about God.

2) We have fun learning about all kinds of things.

3) The people at Sunday school treat us like family.

4) They teach you there's more to life than hanging out with the wrong people.

5) The most important thing is that they teach us to stay in school and not to use drugs.

That's why I love Sunday school.

Carlos
age 10

I like Sunday school because it's nice. I get to learn about the Lord. If you trust Him, He will take care of you. And I don't ever want to miss Sunday school. I don't go to Sunday school just to get snacks or prizes. Some people go just for those things, but not me. I go to learn, sing and talk about the Lord.

Monesia
age 12

In order for you to learn and understand more about the Bible, you must go to Sunday school. The Bible will become much clearer for you to understand, even for a small person like me. Sunday school has a great teaching of our Father, Son and Holy Spirit, which I truly learn to love with all my heart and soul.

In Sunday school you learn about how the earth was developed and who was the first man and woman. You learn respect for yourself and others, and it guides your behavior.

Sunday school is my way of getting much closer to God. This is why I love Sunday school so much.

Torsandia
age 9

I like Sunday school because it teaches us the Bible, and I have fun answering questions. I hope that it will be here when I get older and have children of my own so that they can see the goodness of the Lord that is in some people. I enjoy every service I go to.

Thaddeus
age 8

I like Sunday school because it teaches me about the Bible. It also teaches me how to be a good person overall. I like all the people that work there because they treat me like family. I wish there was Sunday school every day.

Joanne
age 6

I come to Saturday Sunday school to hear the Word of God and to listen to Pastor Bill. He teaches you to listen to your parents, to obey them, to respect others and to help others. I love Pastor Bill because he teaches me about things that I do. I used to disrespect my mother, and now I don't. Thank you, Pastor Bill.

Erica
age 12

I like Sunday school's songs because their songs sound interesting, and they sound exciting. I like Sunday school's games because they are fun, and they have neat prizes. I like the preaching because it teaches me about God and the people of the past.

Aaron
age 9

I think Sunday school is good, especially because we get to learn about God and get to meet other children. Everyone is friends and always happy and playing with each other.

Damion
age 7

I like Bill and all the other people, and I like to go because I like to learn more about Jesus and God, and I like to play games and sing songs and bring my friends so that they can learn more about God and Jesus.

Maria
age 11

I love Sunday school because they teach us all kinds of good things, like not to use drugs and to stay in school. They teach us about God and how to have respect for all things. They treat us like human beings. They teach us to have respect for ourselves and for others. Sunday school is also fun and games, but there's a time to play and a time to work.

Robert
age 11

I give thanks to all the people at Sunday school for keeping this church together so that me and other kids could learn about our Savior Jesus Christ. I am so proud to go to Sunday school no matter what others say. I am here to learn, not to be in the street on Saturday and Sunday mornings because you could get hurt out there.

Tracey
age 11

I like Sunday school because you learn about Jesus and His people.

Shauna
age 6

I don't come just for food. I come for God. And I don't come to talk. I come to talk about God and learn about God. I like Bill and the others, and they are very kind.

Kiana
age 10

WHOSE CHILD IS THIS?

WHOSE
CHILD
IS THIS?

BILL WILSON

WHOSE CHILD IS THIS? by Bill Wilson
Published by Creation House
Strang Communications Company
600 Rinehart Road
Lake Mary, FL 32746
Web sites: www.creationhouse.com
www.charismalife.com

Unless otherwise noted, all Scripture quotations are from the New King James Version of the Bible. Copyright © 1979, 1980, 1982 by Thomas Nelson, Inc., publishers. Used by permission.

Scripture quotations marked KJV are from the King James Version of the Bible.

Scripture quotations marked TLB are from The Living Bible. Copyright © 1971. Used by permission of Tyndale House Publishers, Inc., Wheaton, IL 60189. All rights reserved.

Library of Congress Catalog Card Number: 92-73343
International Standard Book Number: 0-88419-382-9 (paper)

9 0 1 2 3 4 5 BBG 11 10 9 8 7 6
Printed in the United States of America

*There have been so many people to whom
I am eternally grateful for their friendship and
support. I am indebted to them all. Nevertheless, this
dedication is out of appreciation to the one man who
first made the investment and opened a door for me
that would have otherwise remained closed—David
Rudenis. As you read through the book you will
understand how Dave's love and sensitivity for a boy
who was literally a nobody paved the way for my
personal salvation. He also set the example of care
and concern that I was to follow for the rest of my life.
Without question I dedicate this book,* Whose Child
Is This?, *to the man whose child in many ways I
became. Thank you, my friend. Your investment has
borne fruit and will continue to do so for
generations to come. I love you.*

ACKNOWLEDGMENTS

WHEN I FIRST came to New York in 1979 I never dreamed how many people would give sacrificially to help make Metro's inner-city ministry possible. Some have given money; others have donated goods and services; a few have come to live and work in the city beside me. Their sacrifices have made the difference between life and death for thousands of children in New York. Without them this book would never have been written.

I am also grateful to Steve Strang and Creation House for their determination to make this book a reality and to Neil Eskelin for his help in the writing of the manuscript. Many thanks also go to Lisa Dolab and the staff of Metro Church as they waded through stacks of manuscripts, pictures and letters for the book.

And last, my deep appreciation to Tommy Barnett for his true friendship and encouragement at the times when I needed it most.

CONTENTS

FOREWORD

YEARS AGO, WHEN I first started pastoring after many years in the evangelistic field, I felt a strong burden for America's largest cities. Foremost in my mind was New York City—an untapped field brimming with people who needed the Lord. My heart yearned for a great work for God in an area that most Christians had forgotten about—an area where no one wanted to go.

Not too long after that vision, a young man with incredible energy and an uncommon determination became the director of our bus ministry at Westside Assembly of God in Davenport, Iowa. Instantly I knew there was something special about Bill Wilson. The characteristics that differentiated him then have matured to become the hallmarks of his powerful ministry in Brooklyn, New York, today. His intense drive, counterbalanced by deep compassion and an unusual concern for each individual, has enabled Bill not only to discover and cross one of America's last frontiers but to settle it with stability among pressures that, for most people, would be too great to bear.

Bill Wilson has gone where nobody wanted to go and established himself as an enduring pioneer. The wonderful results evident in his ministry are not temporary; while others have come and gone, he has withstood the test of time. A great discipler in his own right, Bill has trained up young men who are preaching all over the world today for the glory of the Lord Jesus Christ. Truly a leader, Bill is not only a worker but an outstanding motivator, not only a thinker but a great communicator with the rare ability and God-given anointing to stir people up with life-changing effects.

Whose Child Is This? is a requirement for the bookshelf of every individual wanting to do something great for God. As you learn from Bill's pioneering and compassionate heart, your own heart will be taken hold of, squeezed and wrung out. And just when you feel you've had enough, it will be squeezed some more.

Prepare yourself for a challenging journey into the life of a man whom I unhesitatingly classify as a genius in Christian leadership today. I thank God that the vision He placed on my heart more than twenty years ago has found its reality in the work of Bill Wilson. Enter into *Whose Child Is This?* with an open heart and an open mind and expect your vision to be expanded in a mighty way.

—*TOMMY BARNETT*
FIRST ASSEMBLY OF GOD
PHOENIX, ARIZONA

A WORD FROM THE PUBLISHER

I 'LL NEVER FORGET the first time I met Bill Wilson. It was an August day in 1977, just days after Elvis Presley died. I was attending a denominational meeting in Oklahoma City, and Elvis's death was the topic of discussion as I sat in a restaurant with several ministers. When a thin young man with shoulder-length hair walked up, someone introduced this unlikely looking fellow as Bill Wilson—the youth pastor responsible for the incredibly successful bus ministry at Tommy Barnett's church in Davenport, Iowa.

Three years later, Bill's passion for reaching kids took him from America's heartland to the Bedford-Stuyvesant area of Brooklyn, New York—a ghetto called "the war zone" by cabbies who refuse to drive there. During the next decade, I kept hearing amazing reports of his success at Metro Church—and we even covered his innovative inner-city ministry in *Charisma* magazine. But I never had much interaction with him personally until 1990 when I heard him speak in Indianapolis at the North American Congress of the Holy Spirit and World Evangelization.

That August, thirteen years after our first meeting, Bill was a featured speaker in one of the evening sessions. He seemed ill at ease on sharing the spotlight with some of the best-known charismatic speakers in the country. But as he spoke from his heart about his ministry in Brooklyn, the twenty-five thousand people there were deeply moved.

Bill's message came at a time when the Lord was awakening in me a renewed interest in Christian education. After fifteen years of publishing Christian magazines, I was sensing a new awareness of the need to reach the next generation with the gospel. I was also experiencing a growing frustration because I saw so little concern for young people on the part of Christians who considered themselves Spirit-filled.

As I listened to Bill that night, my eyes were opened to the enormity of the challenge, and I caught a vision of the opportunity that lay before us.

The deterioration of values in our culture and the break-up of the home have produced an entire generation of hurting, forgotten, often throwaway children. And our self-absorbed society seems to have little time or interest in doing anything to address the needs of this troubled generation.

This lack of interest in the children is even evident in the churches. Too often, the children's ministry is little more than a baby-sitting program designed to entertain the kids while adults enjoy the worship service. Typically the children's ministry is the lowest priority after the main service, the youth ministry, the music ministry and so forth. Many churches—even charismatic churches—no longer have a training program called Sunday school.

Contrast this to Bill Wilson's vision of Christian education. Not only does he bus thousands of children to Metro Church for Sunday school on Sunday, but he also buses them all day Saturday and during the week, too.

He's even developed a concept called "Sidewalk Sunday School" to reach young people in parts of New York City that are far from the church. Bill and his staff use portable stages rigged onto old customized trucks to take these Sidewalk Sunday Schools to children in some of the most dangerous areas of New York. Despite nearly insurmountable obstacles, Metro Church reaches more than eleven thousand children with the gospel each week.

My own interest in Sunday school dates back to my childhood. Growing up in a pentecostal household, I had perfect attendance at Sunday school—and I had the little attendance bars to prove it. In my small church, Sunday school seemed more important than the main service—at least it was better attended. At that time, just about every church that could afford a school bus had a "bus ministry" to bring kids to church. Sunday school was important, or so it seemed.

But things change. As the Charismatic Renewal swept over the church, a new emphasis developed on Bible teaching—instead of preaching—from the pulpit. Many pastors thought the congregation received all the Bible teaching they needed in the main service, so there was little need for a traditional Sunday school. Some churches that came into renewal, in their eagerness for the new and fresh, threw out anything that was done before they entered into the fullness of the Spirit—and that often included Sunday school.

Like many others, Jamie Buckingham's Tabernacle Church in Melbourne, Florida, did away with Sunday school. But in the late 1980s, Jamie began a new emphasis on Christian education—an indication the pendulum was beginning to swing back the other way.

A turning point for Jamie Buckingham came when he realized that most of the young people in his church didn't even know the names of the sixty-six books of the Bible—in fact, he doubted that many adults in his church could recite them. He lamented that so many were ignorant of the basics of the Christian faith— things he had learned in Sunday school.

In "A Vision for Christian Education," a 1989 editorial I wrote in *Charisma* magazine, I used Jamie's experience to raise some important questions: "Of course the issue is deeper than just knowing the books of the Bible or a few Scripture verses. The heart of the matter concerns our attitude toward Christian education. How well are we training not only our youth but also the adults? How well-versed are our people in the things of the Lord? Do they have any knowledge of the major themes and the basic doctrines of the Bible? Do they have any sense of God moving in history?"

My search to answer those questions, coupled with the sense of urgency communicated by Bill Wilson's message at Indianapolis in

1990, eventually led me to a renewed commitment to Christian education. I decided that I would do what I could to train a new generation to minister in the Holy Spirit's power by publishing materials for Spirit-filled churches under the name CharismaLife.

In this endeavor, Bill Wilson has been both a practical help and a source of inspiration. He has developed some materials to use in churches through CharismaLife Publishers. These were tested and proven in the crucible of his ministry in the Bedford-Stuyvesant area of Brooklyn. (If you would like more information about how you can use these excellent materials in your church, write: CharismaLife Publishers, 600 Rinehart Road, Lake Mary, FL 32746.)

In November 1990, Bill accepted an invitation to speak at our first CharismaLife conference. That same week the newspapers were full of stories about snipers who were randomly killing people in New York City. Tragically, one victim was a little girl who was shot as she waited for the bus to take her to Metro Church.

In obvious pain over the loss of one of his kids, Bill struggled to maintain his composure as he addressed the conference. As he shared from his heart, something powerful happened to the crowd—our hearts were joined with his. From that moment, the conference ceased being a place just to get information. Instead, CharismaLife became a facility for forging a new, united vision of reaching a generation for Christ.

Unlike so many others, Bill doesn't just talk about reaching kids; he actually does it. But he's also able to reach adults, helping us to see that the problems of the ghetto—drugs, hopelessness, teen pregnancy, violent crime—are the problems plaguing our entire society. In addition to helping us recognize the tremendous need, he challenges us that each Christian can make a difference—whether we live in the inner city or the suburbs.

Although others in the church and even society at large have lamented the mounting problems and pressures facing us as we approach the twenty-first century, who is stepping forward to offer solutions? Not many. More important, who is willing to pay the price to save a generation at risk? Very few.

Bill Wilson is an exception. His church is making such a difference in Brooklyn that it was honored as *Guideposts* magazine

A Word From the Publisher

Church of the Year in 1990. In recognition of his refusal to abandon the kids of the inner city, in 1992 President George Bush appointed Bill to the Commission on America's Urban Families. Of the eight distinguished members appointed to that panel, only Bill lived in the ghetto. And though he continues to be very involved with the commission, Bill stepped down from the panel because he didn't want to take too much time away from his kids.

It's this intense commitment to see children's lives transformed by Christ that makes Bill Wilson special. It's the reason I asked Bill to write his story.

This is a book about a man who is living out his vision in one of the toughest neighborhoods in America. But it's also a book about the urgent need to share the love of Christ with the next generation. That's ultimately the purpose for telling Bill's story: to plead the children's cause and to encourage Christians to get involved in reaching and teaching young people.

As we finished this manuscript and made final changes, I asked Bill if he was happy with the finished product. He said he was. In fact, he said he could look anyone in the eye and say they should read this book.

On a hot August night in 1990, Bill Wilson's story changed my life by changing the way I viewed the next generation. You should read his story and share it with your friends. It may change your lives, too.

—STEPHEN STRANG
PUBLISHER AND FOUNDER, *CHARISMA* MAGAZINE

The hostile nature of the streets contrasts sharply with the faces of the kids who call this neighborhood home.

CHAPTER ONE

The Blue Picnic Cooler

W HEN I SAW the headline of the final edition of the *New York Daily News,* I just froze. The bold type read "WHO IS SHE?"

Beneath those words was a hand-drawn sketch of a young girl with long black hair. Her eyes were dark and haunting; her brow was furrowed.

The only identity was her morgue case number: M91-5935. She weighed only twenty-five pounds, and it was determined that she was four years old. The girl was discovered by construction workers along the highway at the edge of Harlem—her severely decomposed body stuffed in a picnic cooler. She was nude. Her hands and feet were bound with a cord. Her hair was in a ponytail.

"That's just a stone's throw from one of our Sidewalk Sunday School locations," I said to myself as I stared at the front page.

Her life and death were a mystery. They said she had been dead for at least a week. Her tiny body was curled into a fetal position inside a green garbage bag that had been forced into a blue picnic cooler.

New York's chief of detectives, Joseph Borrelli, knew only one thing for certain. "Her face showed an awful lot of misery and suffering for a person who's only lived four years," he said.

Whose child is this? I wondered.

1

Whose Child Is This?

Not a Pretty Picture

THE GIRL WAS just another statistic to this crime-hardened city, but to me she was much more. At one time she had been a real person who probably liked to play with her dolls and watch cartoons. She was also symbolic of the utter despair that hangs like a thick cloud over our nation's ghettos.

My eyes filled with tears as I put down the paper. She was the reason I had come to this godforsaken city. Day after day, for more than a decade, I had poured every ounce of my life into rescuing such a child. Was there a chance we had somehow reached her? Was she among the more than ten thousand who had come to our Sunday schools the week she was murdered?

Lord, I thought, *is there something more I could have done?*

I walked out of my office and stood on the curb at the corner of Evergreen and Grove in the Bushwick/Bedford-Stuyvesant area of Brooklyn, looking around at the grim realities of life in the ghetto. It is not a pretty picture.

Looking down the block you see drug-infested brownstones and tenement houses. Rusty skeletons of vandalized cars languish on vacant lots. Garbage is piled high—broken bottles and dirty vials that once held crack scattered in the rubble. From this same spot over the years I have seen dozens of people shot, stabbed and scavenged. Just twenty feet down the street two men were killed—right in front of one of our staff members, who was unable to help the victim. No one was arrested, and not a word of the incident appeared in the city's newspapers.

I am continually amazed by what I see. One New Year's Eve I looked out my window and saw some young men lying in the street, daring cars to run over them. On the corner I could see the actual fire coming out of the barrels of guns as they were being fired at random. A police helicopter was circling and hovering overhead, shining its searchlight down on the scene of yet another crime.

The Blue Picnic Cooler
Organized Chaos

DIRECTLY ACROSS THE street is Metro Church, the repaired remains of a former Rheingold brewery, where I am the unlikely pastor. I suppose you could call it safe. It's protected by steel doors, industrial padlocks and coils of razor wire.

Today this corner may look like the leftovers from a time in history most people would rather choose to forget, but on Saturday and Sunday it becomes the most exciting place you can imagine. I would not want to be anywhere else. Huge buses—we have more than fifty of them—arrive at almost the same time. Each is jammed with kids who have waited all week to be here.

At 9:45 on Saturday morning the auditorium is empty. But fifteen minutes later it is filled wall to wall with young people between the ages of five and twelve, ready to soak in everything like sponges. I begin by grabbing the microphone and shouting/singing: "Tell me, whose side are you leaning on?" They sing back the answer at the top of their lungs: "I'm leaning on the Lord's side!"

For the next hour and a half these kids experience a Sunday school that many have described as the only positive thing that these kids have in their lives. Every minute is carefully crafted to present one single concept or truth—through a live band, bigger-than-life cartoon characters, video projectors, skits, games, contests, prizes and a straight-as-an-arrow message. One minute it is sheer bedlam; the next it is so quiet I can whisper and be heard at the top of the farthest bleachers.

At 11:30 A.M. the smiling youngsters run to their designated buses and sing their way back to their squalid tenements and high rises. At 1:00 P.M. and 4:00 P.M. the same thing happens again. We also have two services on Sunday and Sidewalk Sunday Schools, which are the same style of one-hour, fast-paced sessions conducted on weekdays after school from Harlem to the South Bronx.

I still have to pinch myself to believe that this ghetto corner marks one of America's largest Sunday schools with a staff of more than one hundred full-time workers and more than three hundred volunteers. *Guideposts* magazine named it Church of the

Whose Child Is This?

Year. I was also amazed to be invited by President Bush to serve on the National Commission on America's Urban Families.

According to Numbers

WHEN YOU LOOK at the facts in years past, you begin to understand the enormity of the challenge we face. In Brooklyn, South Bronx, Harlem and the areas in which we minister:

- Over 100,000 cars a year are stolen in New York City.
- Unemployment is five times higher than the national average.
- 83 percent of high school freshmen will drop out before graduation.
- Between 60 and 70 percent of the population receives welfare.
- New York Family Court recorded more than twenty-four thousand child abuse petitions last year, an increase of more than 700 percent in the past decade.

But the escalating problems of children and youth are not limited to New York. They are in cities everywhere.

- In American cities more than 30 percent of the population lives below the official poverty line.
- Minority children are far more likely to be poor. Forty-five percent of blacks and 39 percent of Hispanic children are living below the poverty line.
- There are now more than 100,000 homeless children in America.
- On an average day 135,000 students bring guns to U.S. schools.
- There are more than four million teenage alcoholics in our nation.
- Alcohol-related accidents are the leading cause of death among teenagers.
- Every year a million teenage girls become pregnant.

- More than 2.5 million adolescents contract a sexually transmitted disease each year.
- More than a million young people are regular users of drugs.
- One out of every ten newborns in the U.S. is exposed to one or more illicit drugs in the womb.

As I travel around the nation, people corner me and ask, "Why are cities like New York in such a mess?"

I'd like to give a quick answer, but the ghetto isn't what it is just because of one or two problems. It is a combination of factors so frustrating that it reminds me of the juggler in the Chinese circus who spins plates on the ends of sticks. About the time he gets them all spinning, he has to run back to the start of the line to keep the first one going. We are constantly being juggled from one crisis to another. It is part of living here.

What I do know is that New York is a paradox of great contrasts and contradictions. There are five boroughs broken down into dramatically diverse neighborhoods, each with its own distinct personality. There are the very rich and the very poor. The bulk of the middle class has been driven out by everything from economic pressure to the fear of crime. As a matter of fact, Staten Island, the last predominately middle-class borough, is trying its best to secede from the rest of the city. It is just fed up.

"It's Christmas Time!"

BROOKLYN CAN POINT to certain historic events that have transformed a decent neighborhood of hard workers into a slum. First there were the race riots in the 1960s. But what many people remember clearly was a freak electrical blackout in the summer of 1977 that put Brooklyn in the dark for forty-eight hours.

It was like lighting a fuse on a social powder keg. It was actually a model for the L.A. riots. Rioters smashed their way into more than one thousand stores. Legions of looters hauled away everything from frozen turkeys to television sets—anything that wasn't bolted down. Those who felt they didn't get enough doused floors with gasoline and topped them off with lighted matches.

Brand-new cars were driven out through plate glass showroom windows.

Packs of men, women, teens and children ran through the streets with their arms loaded, yelling, "It's Christmas time! It's Christmas time!"

Police cars were overturned and set on fire. Rocks and garbage were thrown at firefighters, forcing them to retreat. Many of the ravaged neighborhoods have never been rebuilt. Instead they are claimed by drug dealers and other criminal elements of society. The streets are so bleak that New York has been called "Calcutta without the cows."

Historically, we've had half a million homeless people, a robbery every six minutes and an AIDS epidemic that is growing increasingly out of control. Many say, "Why even bother?"

Many people look at the poverty in sections of New York and in economically depressed areas across America and shrug their shoulders. "Poverty in this country is practically nonexistent when you compare it to the rest of the world," they say. "Our poor have television sets, telephones and apartments, and they are supported by a federal safety net."

Financial poverty may be more acute in some Third World countries, but in America other devastating pressures are at work—pressures that strike at the very foundation of society and produce the violence that is unique to the American inner cities.

Poor people in the U.S. are far different from those in a Third World nation because of our advanced industrial system. When residents of the ghetto need food, they cannot slaughter their sheep or harvest grain. They must find a supermarket where they are given food in exchange for either food stamps or cash. The destitute ghetto dweller pays the same price as a millionaire—one that guarantees a profit to the producer, the wholesale distributor and the grocery store owner. Actually the ghetto dweller pays *more*. The store owners can charge what they want as they are guaranteed the business. Most ghetto dwellers do not have the luxury of shopping around for bargains because they have no transportation to get out of their neighborhood.

A ghetto-dwelling American in need of shelter cannot pitch a tent in a public park or erect a plywood lean-to on a vacant lot, which is what the poor can do in many foreign countries. Many, including me, have tried doing this in New York and have been either thrown out or beaten with clubs by the local police.

The American poor must live in apartments that comply with local housing codes. It requires a tremendous amount of money. The rent for the substandard apartments in our neighborhood ranges from $350 to $800 a month, which is totally out of reach for most folks. If federal and local rent subsidy funds were cut off, there would be total panic.

The very nature of the system breeds an animosity that just doesn't go away. When you are close enough to touch something but know you just can't reach it, the feelings of frustration and hopelessness build steadily. After several generations of living like this, the entire value system of these people is bankrupt.

Recently, in front of a restaurant where I often eat breakfast, a woman was stomped to death on the sidewalk. Then someone else came over and stole her sneakers. Around the corner from there a young man, with whom one of our staff members had been dealing about the Lord, was shot three times—killed for no apparent reason.

"A Warning to Other Kids"

WE ARE SURROUNDED by nearly nine million people, yet children are starved for love and affection. When Billy Graham spoke to 250,000 people in Central Park in 1991, he said, "New York City is the loneliest place in the world." It was something I knew firsthand.

A short time ago we received a telephone call from a distraught young woman who asked me to conduct her funeral. The teenage girl was dying of AIDS. Within a week she was dead.

Since living in New York I have made it a policy to view the body of the person whom I am burying. The night before the service I went to the morgue, where an assistant mortician ushered me into the room where her body was. He put on a pair of gloves and slowly unzipped the two body bags that held her body. When I saw the form, I wished I had never made that policy.

Whose Child Is This?

Her head was the size of my fist. One ear was totally gone. So were both eyes and the nose. I thanked the man and found the nearest exit. Without question it was the most horrible sight I had ever seen. The virus had totally destroyed her physical body almost beyond recognition.

The dead girl's sister wanted the funeral to be held at Metro Church as well. "I want this to be a warning to other kids," she said.

The girl had attended our Sunday school when she was very young but had chosen not to live her life for Christ. It was the wrong decision. Just before she slipped into unconsciousness, however, she remembered what she had learned in church and made her peace with God. She wanted others to know that this is what happens when you fail to live for the Lord.

You can talk to almost any child in Brooklyn and be shocked to hear stories of how drugs have affected their families.

When crack cocaine flooded the market in the mid-1980s, it became the drug of choice for hundreds of thousands of people in New York.

We are only now dealing with the first wave of "crack babies," children born to mothers who used crack during pregnancy.

I've seen these innocent offspring. Some are like rag dolls, unable either to sit or stand in their own strength. Many are born deaf. Some three-year-olds function like babies of four months. Some are merely a bundle of bones. Their emotions range from passive, to moody, to aggressive, to out of control.

I've talked with several doctors, and they are at a loss for answers. Cocaine in the mother reduces oxygen to the child's brain, which causes physical deformities and damage to the brain and nerves. Babies are sometimes born with unusually small heads. It is a tragic generation.

A mother in the Bronx held her seven-year-old daughter on the floor so a drug dealer could rape her in exchange for three vials of crack.

A drug-addicted mother and father offered their two daughters, two and five years old, to a husband and wife on our staff. They wanted money to buy drugs that day. Knowing someone would take these girls and not wanting even to think about what

8

would happen to them then, our staff members literally bought those two precious girls and raised them for three years in their apartment along with four of their own kids.

"Average" youngsters in our neighborhoods face odds that are stacked against them. By the ages of twelve and fourteen many young men will be heavy drinkers, personal drug users and in trouble with the law. Many girls will become pregnant and trapped in the never-ending cycle of poverty and despair. Children having children—it doesn't make sense. But most things here don't.

Mushrooms and Baby Mules

THE STREETS OF the ghetto define a totally unique environment. The ghetto even has its own vocabulary. *Mushrooms,* for example, is the street word used to describe children who pop up in the line of fire between warring groups and get shot. *Firecrackers* is the word preschool and kindergarten teachers use as a signal for students to hit the floors in case shooting starts outside their classrooms. *Baby mules* is the term used by drug dealers to describe the children they use to carry their drugs and weapons.

When new workers come to New York to join our ministry staff, they are overwhelmed by culture shock. Many are so moved by someone's personal tragedy that they dig into their wallets or purses and offer to help.

One new staffer took a woman to the grocery store and bought her more than sixty dollars' worth of food. A short time later the worker went to the subway station and couldn't believe what she saw. There was that same woman selling the groceries on the street for cash.

I should have warned her. One Thanksgiving we gave away turkeys to kids whose families we knew were in need of food. On the next corner we saw some of the parents selling the turkeys.

Shortly after beginning our ministry in Brooklyn we gave copies of the New Testament to all the kids at Sunday school. The next week some of the kids came up to me crying. Their parents were ripping the pages out of the Bibles to use them as rolling paper for marijuana. It was just the kind of paper they wanted.

Whose Child Is This?

The children we deal with week after week have few choices in life. They don't play organized sports in school because the competition led to violence that was uncontrollable. You'd also have a hard time finding debate teams, tennis clubs or marching bands in the high schools.

Instead the children play in the hallways and stairwells of burned-out buildings, or they play handball in the streets. Cap-and-gown graduations are held in many public elementary schools because they know the majority of kids will never make it through high school.

Fenced in by Fear

GROWING UP IN the shadow of Wall Street and Manhattan's wealthy skyscrapers results in total frustration for a ghetto teen. Television advertisements exploit young men by telling them that they are nobodies without $130 sneakers and $350 leather jackets. Those same teens are living in crowded apartments with no training, no work and no future. It can lead to unfortunate decisions. They think that getting a fast five hundred dollars can bring instant success and recognition.

Ronald Alden, a professor at Northwestern University, says, "The kids selling drugs on the streets are driven by the fact that they have no skills and no access to jobs, and even if they did, they know those jobs only pay half as much money as they can earn selling drugs."

Why don't the people leave? Where would they go? They are fenced in by fear, desperation and a lack of role models.

Anxiety is the constant companion of those who live in the ghetto. They never know what is coming next. There is also despair. It is difficult to find hope when you share your bed with three, and sometimes four, other people. I have visited some apartments where people sleep in shifts because there are not enough mattresses to go around. The plumbing seldom works—nor does the heating.

What about role models? They are hard to find. More than 70 percent of the families in our area are headed by single mothers.

10

Most of the children have never seen their fathers. If they do, the fathers are more often than not hanging out on the corner getting high or getting drunk.

There are also few examples of success—few healthy patterns to follow. The girls look forward to the day when they can have babies and start drawing their own welfare checks.

On a hot summer afternoon you can look up at any tenement building and see mothers leaning out window after window with their arms propped on pillows. They sit there by the hour, just watching. What they see on the street below is far more fascinating than any television soap opera. They get a daily documentary about life and death.

The longer I live here the more I realize that, to many people, humanity has very little value. I was visiting on my bus route on a Friday afternoon and walked through an empty lot; by chance I looked into an open trash bag. Inside I saw the body of a three-week-old baby, discarded like an old doll. Nobody cares. When the death of a child is on the evening news, the typical response is to change the channel.

Attack on DeKalb

I CAN STILL remember the frantic call I received late one night at the church. "Bill, you've got to come over here fast. Our bus captain has just been attacked. She's up on top of an apartment building here on DeKalb Avenue."

I knew exactly where it was and rushed to the scene as fast as I could. The call was from one of the two young people who had been helping her while they visited kids who would be riding the bus the next day.

Three guys jumped the bus captain, and the helpers just ran. The "homeboys" were nineteen or twenty years old. They dragged her to the top of the apartment building and raped her.

The Emergency Medical Service ambulance wouldn't come because they require a police escort in such a building, and the police didn't respond. That left it up to me. I had no other choice but to go after her.

Whose Child Is This?

Her attackers had already left by the time I reached the top of the building and found her curled up in the corner of the building's flat roof. Her clothes were ripped to pieces. Blood was trickling down her face. I will never forget it. I can close my eyes and still see her as clear as I saw her that night. It never goes away.

When you live day after day in an atmosphere of conflict and violence, you think it will never happen to you. But it does. It's not a matter of *if;* it's just *when.*

In my early days in Brooklyn I was walking through one of our bus route neighborhoods. I made the mistake of looking down at the sidewalk instead of looking at a group of guys ahead of me. I wasn't thinking.

When I glanced up they were about a quarter of a block ahead, just standing there, motionless. They were glaring at me. I thought, *Oh, oh,* and quickly rehearsed my options.

If I crossed the street I'd really look stupid because I had obviously set my course. So I thought, *Let me try to just walk through them and not pay attention.*

It didn't work. With every step I knew they weren't going to move an inch. As I tried to find a way through, one of them pushed me and said, "Give up the money."

His buddy pulled out a knife. When I told them I didn't have any money, they didn't believe me; but it was true. I never carry cash on the street.

When I tried to back up, they began beating me with the most powerful blows they could muster. I was way outnumbered. The fellow with the knife stabbed it into my arm, and the blood flowed. Then, just as quickly as they had surrounded me, the fellows turned and walked away briskly.

Is it worth it? I wondered.

A Human Torch?

ONE EVENING I was walking back to my apartment after visiting children in their tenements. Six older teenagers surrounded me without any warning and grabbed my arms. One of them held a can of gasoline and another a cigarette lighter.

Before they could douse my clothes and turn me into a human torch, a boy yelled out something in Spanish from a nearby building. To this day I don't know what he said, but the gang suddenly stopped and walked away as if nothing had happened. I can only give God the glory for watching over me as He did that day.

After a few such confrontations you develop a street sense—a perception of what is happening all around you—always watching, ready to react instantly to the slightest sign of danger. Losing concentration can be deadly. Most outsiders never stay around that long to learn. It takes time.

People new to the ghettos of New York are intrigued by the elaborate murals painted by street artists on the brick walls of abandoned buildings. It's an art form all its own, with thick, colorful letters and designs sprayed from aerosol cans and markers.

They often mark the spot where someone was killed.

Behind every scene is a story. Often the words will read something like what I saw last week in a mural near the corner of Hart and Irving: "In memory of Pito. Mom and Dad love you." The dates of birth and death painted at the bottom of the poignant marker indicated the boy was only seventeen.

When someone is killed on the streets, the painting is a memorial—perhaps the only recognition they ever received. But it is only temporary. After the next shooting it will be painted over with, "God bless [the name of the latest victim]"—and maybe a different picture.

I've seen hundreds and hundreds of graffiti memorials to "nobodies" who wanted to be "somebodies."

A Crash at the Cemetery

I WILL NEVER forget being asked to conduct the funeral of a young Puerto Rican boy who was a victim of a drug deal gone wrong. His parents were Christians and turned to me during this unfortunate time.

At the burial plot, after a few words and a prayer, the beautiful metal casket was lowered into the ground, and we began to walk away. Moments later I heard loud crashing sounds coming from behind where I was standing. As I turned around I was stunned to see members of the family standing near the hole in the ground, throwing rocks at the casket. I walked back to the grave and was astonished to see huge dents on top of the beautiful casket.

Were they angry at the boy? I wondered. I was totally confused by the whole scene.

"What is happening?" I asked.

"Please don't worry about it, Pastor," they said. "If we don't do this, the funeral directors will come back tonight and put his body in a wooden box and clean the casket off and sell the casket to someone else."

I learned that the cemetery owner makes extra money by cutting such a deal with the funeral home. They will resell the same casket over and over again.

I have spent many sleepless nights staring out the window of my apartment asking the same questions: *Is it worth the hassle? Am I wasting my time? Does anybody really care?*

But then I think about walking up four flights of urine-scented stairs to remind a little boy to be ready for my Sunday school bus. He is a six-year-old named Tyrone. Suddenly the door springs open, and he runs for me at top speed. He leaps into my arms saying, "Pastor Bill! Pastor Bill!" He squeezes my neck as if he never wants to let go.

What if I were not there? What if the bus never came? What if he didn't have the chance to hear a message of hope?

The lessons we have learned are not just for Bushwick or Harlem. They are for an abandoned generation across America— from Boston to Burbank. In this book you will see that the ways we reach children in New York City can be modified to reach the children where you live. And we've got to start reaching them.

The public school system has forsaken the children by failing to teach the basic values and principles of life. Parents have abandoned them to *Sesame Street,* Saturday morning cartoons and, unfortunately, programs or videos you and I would be embarrassed to look at. The church has neglected them through irrelevant and outdated programs.

After spending thousands of hours "in the trenches," I am

convinced that a major revolution is needed in the training of America's children.

Building prisons and rehabilitation centers is not the answer—it's like placing a Band-Aid on a cancer. We've got to reach them when they are young. It's the continuing Christian controversy of prevention vs. intervention. We usually wait till it's too late then get concerned. It's the question, Do we put a fence around the top of the mountain or an ambulance at the bottom?

Whose child is this?

The question must be asked sooner rather than later—and not when the subject is in a blue picnic cooler on the side of the road. Not when someone's child becomes case number M91-5935.

Above: Children anxiously await their turn to get off the bus and go to Sunday school.

Right: Despite his busy schedule, Bill Wilson still drives his route whenever possible.

CHAPTER TWO

"You Wait Here"

I WAS FOURTEEN years old. My mother and I were walking down the street on the block where we lived in Pinellas Park, Florida—just north of St. Petersburg. It was near the Welcome Inn on Park Boulevard, where she worked as a barmaid.

We stopped and sat down on a concrete culvert that was built over a little drainage ditch. She was very quiet that day. After a few minutes she stood up and said, "I can't do this anymore. You wait here." *What is she talking about?* I wondered. *What is it she can't do anymore?*

I did exactly what my mom said. I sat there waiting for her to return. The sun went down, and she still wasn't back.

The next day I sat on that same culvert, alone with my thoughts. I knew it was a difficult time for my mom and dad. Life had not been easy.

I was born when they lived in South Boston. Dad found work driving a bus, but it wasn't enough to support the family. He thought the grass would be greener in San Francisco, so we headed west.

I was twelve when we lived on the West Coast. My sister, Sandy, is eight years older. She was the only stabilizing factor in my life, always doing her best to encourage and protect me. I was a skinny kid who was always the target of some neighborhood bully. More than once she came to my rescue when I thought nobody would.

Whose Child Is This?

But nothing seemed to work out for the Wilson family in San Francisco. Dad announced that we were going to move to Florida because we had some relatives there. However, within a few weeks it was obvious that coming to the Sunshine State was the biggest mistake we could have made. Ours was not a happy home. The family deteriorated to the point that my mother and father divorced. My father had tuberculosis and was a patient in a TB hospital in Tampa.

Where Was Mom?

AS A CHILD I never felt loved by my parents. I can't say I ever really knew my dad. And my mother, to cushion life's blows, had turned her life over to the bottle. She had become an alcoholic.

When she and my dad divorced, her drinking binges became more frequent. She would bring home a different man from the bar nearly every night. These men were the roughest I'd ever seen. Night after night I'd fall asleep to the sounds of cursing, fighting and carousing. One night it became so bad that I found a gun and was ready to shoot my mom's companion. As I sat for the second day on that culvert, I thought about the nights that my mom didn't come home. Was that happening again? Surely she'd be back soon.

For three days I sat in the Florida sun on that hot, concrete culvert. I didn't know where to turn. My sister had married and moved to New Jersey. Dad was gone. If I had known how to pray, I would have done it, but religion had no place in our home.

All I could do was try to be brave and choke back the tears that would fill up my eyes.

Mom never came back.

A man who lived down the street had noticed me sitting in that same spot for the past three days. His name was Dave Rudenis. I had talked with him before and watched him work on his race car at his house. He walked over to me, and we began to talk. He asked if he could get me some food. Dave was an auto mechanic who liked to drive race cars. He was also a deacon at a local church, First Assembly of God, in St. Petersburg.

"How would you like to go to youth camp?" he asked.

"What's that?" I responded.

"Oh, you'd love it. Lots of kids your age will be there. They have softball, swimming and great services." *Services?* I wondered. *What are those?*

Dave Rudenis paid the week's tuition, $17.50, and put me in the pastor's station wagon with some other teens. I was headed for Camp Alafia, which is out in the "boonies" of Central Florida—somewhere between Mulberry and Bradley Junction.

No Longer Alone

BY NATURE I was a loner—partly because I didn't know how to relate to other people and partly because of my horrible self-image. I wasn't just tall and thin—I was skinny. My teeth protruded, my jaw was visibly disfigured and I always had holes in my pants.

I kept to myself most of the time, but on Wednesday night at that camp I heard something that totally changed my life. For the first time I listened to the simple story of how Jesus died on a cross for me—and that He rose again so I could spend eternity with Him.

I don't remember who the camp speaker was or the title of his sermon, but that night I walked to the front of the auditorium and found a place to kneel at the left side of the altar. I said, "Jesus, I want You to forgive me of my sin. I want to give my life to You." Somehow I knew that my future would never be the same from that night on. When I returned to St. Petersburg, Dave was waiting for me. He had already heard that I had found the Lord at Camp Alafia.

"Son," he said, "I want you to know how much we love you. Just don't worry. Everything's going to be all right. We'll take care of you."

I'd never heard words like those before.

The next weekend I attended the first Sunday church service of my life. I was seated by myself because I didn't feel comfortable with the other young people. I guess I did look pretty bad, with holes in my pants and with my funny-looking face.

Whose Child Is This?

The song leader said, "Let's turn to page 269 and sing 'Springs of Living Water.'"

I had never sung out of a songbook before. I thought you read a song like you read a book—when you finish one line, you continue with the line right under it. But that's not the way it works!

I was just singing away, not realizing that I wasn't singing what everybody else was. A kind, little old lady was seated behind me. She leaned forward, put her arm on my shoulder and said, "Let me teach you how this goes."

The people at the church were patient with me.

A few days later my father, who had been released from the tuberculosis hospital, died of a heart attack. It was then that two of the most wonderful people who have ever lived invited me into their home and later gave me a place to live at the church. They were Wayne Pitts and his wife, Evelyn. He was the pastor of First Assembly.

Because of my physical appearance I was extremely introverted. My dental structure and jaw disfigurement would take braces, and later surgery, to correct. It was Pastor Pitts and his wife who helped me get my first braces.

The people at the church were more than kind. They actually cared. They even invited me to join Royal Rangers, a youth program for boys. The commander realized how sensitive I was about my appearance and made me feel like part of the group, not an outcast.

At the Phone Booth

AT ROYAL RANGER meetings we learned everything from how to tie knots to how to make a fire without matches. They also taught us the importance of sharing Christ with others. "It's part of the Christian walk," our leader would say. But being a new Christian and extremely shy, I felt totally incapable of doing that. When we would go to pass out gospel tracts, I would almost panic. While no one was looking, I would go off on my own and place the little tracts in phone booths so I wouldn't have to confront anybody.

One day after placing some tracts in an outdoor phone booth, I walked across the street to see if anyone would actually read them. A few minutes later a man entered the booth to make a call.

He also picked up one of the tracts. After looking at it, he put the tract in his pocket and walked away.

I can't begin to express what that one experience did for me. For the first time in my life I realized I could actually influence someone for Christ.

In high school I took a vocational skills track because of my interest in being an auto mechanic just like Dave Rudenis, who had become my hero. I found some part-time work tinkering with old cars, and after graduation I began working at the local Ford Motor Company dealership—and racing cars every chance I got.

The pastor who succeeded Wayne Pitts was Don Rippy. He and his wife, Arthelene, believed in me more than I could understand. Don once said, "Bill, we feel you have the potential to do some great things in your life, and we want to help you."

Don Rippy bought me the first pair of brand-new shoes I could ever remember owning. I was seventeen at the time. He and Arthelene also let me continue to live at the church and encouraged me at every turn. Then one day they came to me and said, "We believe you ought to go to Bible school in Lakeland." They were talking about Southeastern Bible College, operated by the Assemblies of God for the training of ministers and church workers.

"Why should I do that?" I asked. "I'm not planning to be a preacher. I've got a job as an auto mechanic."

Then I thought, *Why not? It can't hurt me.*

Speaking at the Stockade

MY FRESHMAN YEAR was difficult, to say the least. I barely had enough money to scrape by, but what really made it difficult was that I didn't have a clear reason for being there.

On Sunday afternoons some of the students would hold services at the local jail—they called it the "stockade." Week after week they invited me to go along. I always refused with various lame excuses, but the real reason I didn't go was that I had never spoken in public before. Because of my teeth I could not talk clearly, and I was not about to make a fool of myself.

Finally, during my second semester, I relented and joined the group. During a service at the jail one week, the leader said, "Now we want you to meet Bill Wilson, from St. Petersburg. Bill, come and tell these men what is on your heart."

Not much, I thought. My testimony lasted about forty-five seconds. But later that night, as I put my head on my pillow, a big smile came over my face. I knew I had discovered something that I wanted to do again and again.

During my second year at Southeastern, a visiting minister spoke in a chapel service. He said, "God is not looking for people who have ability, but availability. That's all you need." I knew he was talking about me.

When the invitation was given to commit our lives to full-time Christian service, I walked down the aisle for the second time in my life. The first had been at Camp Alafia. This time I again walked down to the left side of the altar, and again—without a lot of fanfare—said, "Lord, if You can use someone like me, I'll do my best." Nobody laid hands on me, and there was no prophecy—just a decision to make a commitment.

When I returned to my home church, Pastor Rippy said, "Bill, how would you like to work part time this summer with our vacation Bible school program?"

"It sounds good to me," I said. "Just tell me what you want me to do."

We set up a big tent in front of the church to give the VBS some neighborhood visibility. A lady in the church, Dagney Johnson, bought a Volkswagen van and donated it so that we could pick up neighborhood children. My job was to drive the van. I had a great time with the children that week.

But after VBS was over, nobody knew what to do with the van. Pastor Rippy approached me and said, "If you can think of a way to use it, fine. If not, we'll sell it."

I noticed that several hundred kids came to vacation Bible school, but only a few would come to church on Sunday. It was then that I began observing what was happening in Sunday school and how it was totally different from VBS. I walked down the halls and listened to what was being taught in class after class. The presentation was boring. I wouldn't want to sit through an hour of it myself.

Would the children attend Sunday school if it were more like what they had experienced in the tent? I wondered about this. We would soon find out.

"Pastor," I said, "can I suggest a few changes in the way we reach some of these kids?"

"You can do whatever you want."

He still believed in me.

Clowns and Cardboard

WE CAME UP with the idea of a network called NBC—Neighborhood Bible Club. I enlisted the help of some teenagers, and we went into an area—an empty field or a corner lot—and set up a colorful platform. We attracted the kids with these outdoor sessions. It was a simple plan. We would teach them a Bible lesson, do our best to interest them in coming to our Sunday school and then do follow-up.

Some of the ladies at the church got out their sewing machines and made clown suits. Then we found a huge cardboard refrigerator box, put a hole in it and painted it with bright colors. We put a little curtain over the opening, and I practiced my Syd and Marty Kroft puppet imitation.

I remember the first day we tried our new puppet experiment. We set the refrigerator box on top of a hill with the children seated on the ground looking up at it. I thought it was a great idea. At a certain time in the program I climbed into the cardboard box to do my puppet routine. But a big gust of wind came along and blew the box over—with me in it. I tumbled down the hill to the screams and delight of the kids. I was embarrassed, but they were all clapping. They thought it was part of the program. At that point most folks would have said, "This just isn't going to work. We must be out of the will of God."

The next day we went back, and I put two concrete blocks in the bottom of the refrigerator box. The crowd grew. The third day, on Friday, more than one hundred children gathered to sing, watch a puppet show, play Bible quiz games and hear a gospel message.

That day I did something I had never done before in my life. I asked the children to accept Jesus into their lives. I was more than surprised to see over half of the children raise their hands. I didn't know what to do next, so I copied what Pastor Rippy did at church. I asked them to bow their heads, and I led them in the sinner's prayer.

Then I asked, "How many of you have enjoyed the Bible club this week?"

Every child raised his or her hand.

"How many of you would come to Sunday school if it were done the same way?"

Again, every hand reached for the sky.

"How many of you would like to ride to Sunday school with me in a Volkswagen van this week?"

They all said yes.

Before they had a chance to change their minds, I said, "If you mean it, line up in single file, and we'll get your names and addresses." The next day was Saturday, so I said, "Tell your parents that tomorrow we'll stop by to see if it is all right for you to ride to Sunday school with us this week."

Our team of volunteers divided up the names and addresses, and we made a personal visit to the home of every one of those children. Most of the families, we learned, had no church affiliation.

That first Sunday we picked up thirty-six children for church and Sunday school. The van came into the church parking lot with two flat tires. It was jampacked, but we were on our way to building a dynamic, soulwinning program for reaching young people.

It was a day that would be permanently circled on the calendar of my life. That Sunday was the birth of a Sunday school ministry that has changed my life and the lives of literally hundreds of thousands of kids all over the world.

"Where the Action Is!"

DURING THE REMAINING months of that summer we continued the Neighborhood Bible Club, the Saturday home visits and the bus routes on Sunday. By September we had more buses and were bringing in almost a hundred children for the Sunday activities.

At that time Pastor Rippy asked, "Bill, do you think it would be possible for you to come home every weekend from college and continue the bus ministry and children's church?" Needless to say, my answer was a resounding *yes*. Besides my joy at the thought of continuing the ministry, an unexpected blessing was that the church paid my travel expenses and also fed me.

Next, First Assembly changed its name to Suncoast Cathedral and put up a building behind the sanctuary specifically for our program. On Easter Sunday in 1969, we bused in 102 children.

We formed a ministry team of older teens to plan, sing, teach and put on puppet shows. They also helped to handle the discipline. We painted a big banner and hung it on one of the walls of the new facility. It read, "This Is Where the Action Is!"

The children's ministry continued to grow and expand. In what seemed like a short time we had twelve buses bringing in six hundred children every week.

When I graduated from Southeastern in 1971, Pastor Rippy asked me to join the staff on a full-time basis.

It was not a dream that came true. But I knew my life was not my own. I was willing to do whatever it took.

I threw myself into the task as if there were no tomorrow. From sunrise until after midnight, seven days a week, I was running at full speed with only one objective—to reach as many kids with the gospel as possible.

One afternoon I literally collapsed on the floor of my office and had to be rushed to the hospital. It was only a minor heart problem, but the doctors told me that I had a heart disease—obviously a hereditary problem that I would have to live with.

Years of also misusing my vocal cords gave my voice a permanent rasp—a scratchy sound that is with me to this day.

While I was at Suncoast Cathedral, a young evangelist by the name of Tommy Barnett came for a revival crusade. He was noted for his illustrated sermons. One afternoon he needed to go to the lumber store to buy some materials to build props for a presentation. He asked if I wanted to go with him.

"I'll be glad to help you," I told him. We built a huge wooden cross for a sermon he was going to present called "The Whip, the Hammer and the Cross."

Whose Child Is This?

That week I quickly gained a tremendous respect for Tommy's drive and creativity for evangelism. Tommy and I had a lot in common when it came to evangelism. In fact, we got to be good friends that week.

Some years later Tommy and I were talking on the phone. He had accepted his first pastorate, in Davenport, Iowa. "I need someone to help with our bus ministry. I think you'd be the perfect one to do it," he said.

"I'll be there," I told him.

"Can You Help Us?"

PASTOR BARNETT HAD already developed one of the fastest-growing Sunday school programs in the nation. For the next five years, on the edge of the cornfields of Iowa, I jumped in and gave it my best. With one of the greatest groups of volunteers I've worked with, many of whom are now in full-time ministry themselves, the bus ministry grew from 450 to 2,000.

During that time calls began to come in from all parts of the country. "Can you come and help us expand our children's program?" asked a pastor in Portland.

"Do you have a manual we can use to start a bus ministry?" wrote a layman from Lansing.

It seemed that every other week I was flying to speak at another how-to-do-it seminar. I was also writing children's church curriculum materials for a company I was part owner in called the Train Depot in Tampa, Florida. The Train Depot became one of the nation's most innovative producers of Sunday school and youth training materials.

Even though the program in Davenport was a huge success, there was a restlessness in my spirit. I knew that God had something else on my agenda. I didn't know where it was or what it was, but my heart was open. I always wanted to do more and believed I could.

Over the years I have learned that God communicates His will in four unique ways: through needs, through circumstances, through relationships and through open doors. I have never been knocked over by an angel, nor have I ever heard the audible voice of God say, "Bill, here is what I want you to do." But He has always made His will clear to me in His time.

Like a Magnet

FOR SEVERAL MONTHS I felt a growing desire to see a vibrant children's ministry develop in the inner cities of our nation. I had visited enough ghettos to know that these kids weren't being reached.

In Davenport Pastor Barnett had developed a training program that brought young people from all parts of the country for hands-on training in building a soulwinning church and Sunday school. One student was from Brooklyn, and he would tell me again and again about life in the city and the need to see lives transformed. He returned to be an associate pastor of a church there.

This was in the late 1970s, and I was spending more and more time training youth workers and Christian education directors around the country.

Whenever possible, I found myself arranging my schedule to be near New York City. I was drawn to it like a magnet. It seemed as if I was there at least once a month. My friend from Brooklyn helped me understand some of the contrasting personalities of the neighborhoods. I rode the subways and walked through high crime areas. What I saw were thousands of young people in deep trouble—their needs not being met by either the church or the government.

During one visit I asked some locals, "What is the worst part of the city?"

They laughed and said, "It's all the worst part."

Names like Harlem, the South Bronx, Bushwick, Bedford-Stuyvesant, Brownsville, the Lower East Side kept coming up in every conversation I had with people here. I had a contact in Bushwick—an area of about two square miles of pure hell—in Brooklyn. It was tougher than anything I'd ever seen.

I couldn't understand it. "Why isn't anybody doing here what I'm doing in Davenport?" It didn't make sense.

"It won't work here," everybody said. But I wasn't buying it.

For several months, no matter where I was or what I was doing,

Whose Child Is This?

I couldn't get New York City out of my thoughts. The need was simply too great.

In 1979 I made the decision to leave Davenport. I didn't have much encouragement, and there was virtually no financial support, but that didn't really matter. I knew I had to go.

I put all of my earthly possessions in a little rented trailer and began driving east until I crossed the Verrazano Bridge into Brooklyn. This was my new home. What a sight. I was looking into the face of poverty, hostility, pain and hunger.

"Lord," I prayed, "I'm going to need Your help with this one!" I had a note in my pocket from a pastor in New York that said, "I'll give you six months, and you'll be gone like everybody else."

"How About Saturday?"

I WAS INTRODUCED to the pastor of a Spanish pentecostal church in the Bushwick area on Menahan Street.

"Can I rent the building?" I asked the minister.

"You can't rent it on Sunday—we have about eleven members who come here for church."

"That's all right. How about Saturday?" I had started the Saturday Sunday school idea back in Iowa, so this prospect wasn't new to me at all.

Teenagers from the neighborhood helped us hand out flyers that first week announcing that Sunday school was coming. Most of the kids didn't know what Sunday school was. They had never heard the words before.

It was a strange sight to the neighborhood. They must have wondered what a long-haired preacher in blue jeans and a T-shirt was doing here. And besides this, I was white.

But before long some Spanish and black Christian young people from the area heard about what we were doing and joined us. With a small nucleus we began to have youth meetings in the evening during the week.

We would divide the teens into four teams for contests. They would compete with each other in pie-eating contests, water-balloon-throwing contests, banana-eating contests or whatever.

The first twenty minutes was just good, clean fun. Then we'd sing lively choruses for twenty minutes, and I'd wind it up with a hard-hitting message and give the young people an opportunity to accept Christ.

Many responded. Week after week the numbers grew. Then I announced that we would be having training sessions for bus workers. That was truly a leap of faith. Bus workers? We didn't even have any buses yet!

I did have a call from a couple of pastors who heard what we were doing, and they said, "We'll give you some old junk buses."

And they did. I think those buses were held together by the paint job alone. They were the kind that had to be cranked over and over to get the engine going. Then once they got started, they wouldn't stop!

Block by Block

WE MAPPED THE area block by block and carefully designed bus routes and time schedules for bringing the children to Sunday school.

At the training sessions we assigned bus captains and assistants for each route. We printed more flyers announcing the first week and sent the teens to their area to start meeting parents and signing up children.

It was obvious that our junk buses wouldn't do the job, so we raised some money to rent buses—complete with drivers—from a local transportation company.

On the first day, in June 1979, we had no idea what to expect. But that Saturday, when the buses rolled in, there was a total of 1,010 kids. We did have a slight problem. The church seated only three hundred. So we kept the other seven hundred outside and brought them inside in shifts. It was one of the happiest night-mares of my life.

A few weeks after we started, the pastor of the church called me to his little office. "The carpet is getting dirtier," he told me.

That is impossible, I thought. *That carpet can't get any dirtier!*

But he allowed us to continue. Then a few weeks later, when our attendance was more than thirteen hundred, he called me in again.

Whose Child Is This?

"We have really got a problem. The kids have broken the fixtures in the bathrooms," he said.

Since the plumbing hadn't worked the whole time we were there, I didn't know what he meant. But I got the message. We were being politely kicked out.

I wondered, *How can you get kicked out of the ghetto? Where do you go from here?*

We were already at the end of the world.

Left: Bill greets the kids with a hug and a friendly smile as they climb on the bus.

CHAPTER THREE

"Sorry, Kids— It's Over"

METRO SUNDAY SCHOOL was "on the move," but not exactly in the way we wanted to be. I had no idea, however, that one day soon I would be standing on the hood of one of our buses, saying, "I'm sorry to tell you this, but this is our last week. *It's over.*"

After the decision was made to leave the Spanish church, I scrambled fast to find a new home for the ministry. "We were kicked out of the pentecostal church," I told the Baptist pastor a few blocks down the street. "Do you think we can rent your building every Saturday?"

"I've seen your buses going by," he said. "Yes. I think it will work. We'd love to have you here."

Attendance continued to grow. Within a few months our numbers had climbed to two thousand. One day the Baptist pastor came to me and said, "The people in our church really like you. In fact, we are having a revival next week, and we would like you to preach the opening service."

I said, "Sure, I'd be honored."

What I didn't tell him was that the children had broken one of the legs of a pew the previous Saturday. The service had been rather enthusiastic, and they must have gotten carried away. It was on the front row on the left-hand side of the church. The wood was totally split. I thought about telling him but remembered how the Spanish pastor reacted whenever something went wrong.

The pew was beyond repair. I nailed it, beat on it and prayed over it, but nothing seemed to help.

I Just Froze

ON SUNDAY MORNING I was seated on the platform, waiting to be introduced. It was a proud moment for our ministry, but I couldn't help glancing nervously at that precarious pew from time to time. A few women were seated there, and I figured maybe it was going to stand the test.

Then, right in the middle of reading my text, I looked up at the back door where a rather large woman had just walked in. She was coming down the middle aisle, and I just froze. And I never freeze. *Please, Lord, don't let her sit on that broken pew,* I thought as I stopped reading the Scriptures.

The whole church must have seen my reaction, because they turned their heads to watch her continue down the aisle. It was like watching a car wreck in slow motion. She took her seat on the end of that pew. The weakened leg gave way, but the other end stayed up.

Well, you should have seen it! The whole row of women slid down the pew and landed in a pile in the center aisle. They were yelling and screaming, and the service was definitely out of control.

I don't have the gift of prophecy, but I knew that we had better start looking for a new home. I thought we might make it a month, but I was wrong. The next week we were on the streets again.

It was two weeks before Christmas, and I took our dilemma to a Brooklyn real estate agent. Because we needed a larger facility, we had a real problem. Most of the warehouses in the area had been burned out or vandalized. Plus, we didn't have the money to repair them even if we could get one. Many buildings were victims of what New Yorkers call "landlord lightning"—where the owner torches the facility to get an insurance settlement.

I reminded the agent, "Since it is winter, we also need something with heat."

"No problem," he said. "I think we've got the perfect building."

We signed the papers for a warehouse on the corner of Broadway and Grove, next to the elevated train tracks that carried passengers into Manhattan. What he didn't know was that the boilers in the building had blown up, and the heaters didn't work. The first Saturday we were there the temperature was seventeen degrees outside—and seventeen degrees inside.

A Cold, Cold Saturday

THE SITUATION WAS worse than you could imagine. Many of the kids came in T-shirts because they didn't own coats. The staff had worked hard to prepare a great program, but we cut it short. We knew those children needed to be back in their homes, or they would be in the hospital with pneumonia.

I wanted to continue, but it was impossible to go on.

I remember very clearly on that cold Saturday in January, I stood on the hood of one of our buses with a battery-operated megaphone and told a sea of faces, "We won't be having Sunday school anymore."

My voice choked, and I said, "Sorry, kids, it's over."

That day was a personal tragedy for me. Earlier I had told the staff of my decision, and we all cried to think that our efforts had led to this. "Isn't there something we can do?" they asked.

We had explored every option and come up blank. Even returning to a small church was out of the question. The program had grown much too large for that. Besides, there wasn't anyone who would have us.

When I climbed down from that bus, I couldn't look those kids in the eyes. I just wanted to get out of there as fast as I could. In my heart I felt like a total failure. "Lord," I said, "I've let the kids down, I've let the staff down and I've let You down. I'm sorry."

You may not understand the impact of what happened, but those children were devastated. For many, Sunday school was all they had. It was the one glimmer of hope in their week—a refuge from their brutal environment. There wasn't anything else. We may not have been much, but we were it.

Almost as quickly as the dream was born, it died.

Where Would I Go?

WHAT SHOULD I do now? I thought. *We don't have a building, and we have very few supporters. I guess I'll rent another trailer and drive out the same way I came in.*

I thought about going back to some church that might need a children's minister, but who would want a failure? I even thought about getting out of the Lord's work altogether. But what would I do? Where would I go? I couldn't bear to think of what it would be like when all my "spiritual" friends came around and said, "I told you so."

Several months went by. I was still traveling although I didn't know why. Every day I wanted to leave. But I stayed.

Where to this Sunday? The destination was Lubbock, Texas. I was to fly there and drive over to a little town called Levelland to speak on Sunday morning. The pastor had invited me to come so that I could present our financial needs to his congregation to help keep our ministry alive.

Alive, I thought. *This work is dead. It's over. After all, that's what I had just told those disappointed children.*

What could I possibly say to that congregation? Maybe I should call the pastor and tell him, "There's no point in wasting your time or mine. I'm going to have to cancel my flight. It's over. We've closed the ministry in Brooklyn."

But one tiny part of me would not let me take that option. I knew the pastor had promoted the service, so I couldn't let him down. I caught a taxi to La Guardia Airport and flew to the Lone Star State.

Early on Sunday morning in Levelland, I turned on the motel room television, and there was Robert Schuller, as confident and positive as ever. I talked back to the television set: "It's easy for you to talk that way. You've got a Crystal Cathedral in Southern California. You should have been with me when I had more than two thousand kids freezing to death in a ghetto warehouse!"

"Sorry, Kids—It's Over"

When I stopped muttering to myself, I sat on the edge of my bed, watching and listening. Schuller was talking about the will of God and the importance of "hanging in there." He talked about discouragement and said, "You know, at times it's just easier to go fishing."

His words were just for me. I fell to my knees and said, "Lord, give me one more chance. I know there's a way for this ministry to survive."

Later that morning I went to the church and told them, "Friends, at times it may look cold and bleak, but we haven't even begun. Tomorrow I'm going back to Brooklyn to give it one more try. We're going to claim the territory and rescue children from hell."

"Sorry, Mister"

THOSE WORDS WERE easy to speak when I was inspired. But when I returned to New York, reality hit fast.

"Where to?" asked the taxi driver at La Guardia.

"Brooklyn," I said.

"Where in Brooklyn?" he wanted to know.

"It's in Bushwick," I told him.

"Sorry, mister. You'll have to find another cab. I don't go there."

After asking three drivers I finally found someone who would drive me home.

Surveying the scene of a boarded-up ministry was almost more than I could handle. In Texas I had found some new strength, but now I was already finding the zeal and enthusiasm draining from me.

As the days and weeks passed, I could not walk one block down a street in the neighborhood without little children running up and asking, "When are we going to have Sunday school again? I miss it so much!"

Even mothers would stop me and say, "You don't know how much those Saturday mornings meant to my children."

The ministry was shut down for almost a year. What I remember

37

most about that time was that every morning when I walked out of my apartment, I wanted to pack my things, put them in the car and go back where I came from. I'd like to tell you God spoke to me audibly, telling me to stay. That would make a good testimony, and it's the right thing to say. But that didn't happen. I can't even tell you why I stayed. I just knew that if you go back, you die. So you just keep trying to go forward.

Then one day a kid who used to go to the Sunday school told me about an old building at the corner of Evergreen Avenue and Grove Street in the neighborhood where we had Sunday school before. I learned it was built in 1926 as a Rheingold brewery. Then it had become a notorious "chop shop"—a place where stolen cars were stripped down and sold as used parts. More recently it was used as a warehouse but was in obvious need of repair.

"How Much Do You Want?"

WHEN I FOUND the man who owned it, I said, "I hear you want to rent the building."

"No, it's for sale."

"We can't buy anything," I said. "We've just got a bunch of poor kids that I'm trying to bring to a Sunday school. I might be able to rent it."

"It's for sale or nothing," he said.

"How much do you want for it?" I asked.

"A hundred and fifty thousand dollars," he replied.

That was a lot of money for a ministry that didn't have any. Then I remembered something Tommy Barnett taught me when we were in Davenport. He said, "Bill, you've got to remember that everything is negotiable. You ask how much something is. If the amount is too high, you say, 'Well, that's not too bad.' And if something is more than one hundred dollars, you can offer to put some money down on it."

"A hundred and fifty thousand dollars?" I asked. "That's not too bad." Then I said, "Let me ask it another way. What is the lowest price you'll take for it?"

"A hundred and fifty thousand dollars," he stated without flinching.

"Well, how much do you want as a down payment?"

"We'll have to have a minimum of twenty-five thousand dollars," he responded.

"Well, that's not too bad," I repeated. "But you have to understand. That's an awful lot of money for a church like ours."

I thanked the man and walked away.

Twenty-five thousand dollars, I thought. *It might just as well be a million.*

At that moment the invisible Metro Church had a grand total of $98.16 in its bank account. That was all! No slush funds. No CDs. Ninety-eight dollars and sixteen cents—that's lunch money and everything.

The next Sunday I was scheduled to speak at another church in Texas—in a town named Tyler.

A Change in Plans

"HELLO? IS THIS Bill Wilson?" asked a lady at the other end of the phone line.

"That's me," I said.

"Well, you don't know me, but my name is Nell Hibbard. I'm the pastor of the Gospel Lighthouse Church in Dallas."

Then she said something that really got my attention. "God woke me up in the middle of the night and said that a man by the name of Bill Wilson was supposed to preach here next Sunday."

She continued, "I don't know a Bill Wilson. But one of our staff members has heard of you. You're the only Bill Wilson we know. You're supposed to be here Sunday," she said.

"I can't," I told her. "I'm supposed to be in Tyler."

"Well, God said you're supposed to be here Sunday, so we'll see you then."

The phone went dead. She had hung up—and that was it!

Immediately I dialed the number of the pastor in Tyler and said, "You'll never believe this, but a lady by the name of Nell

Hibbard just called from Dallas and said I am supposed to preach at her church on Sunday."

He said, "You can't—you're supposed to be here."

I said, "I know that, but she said God told her that I am supposed to be there."

Then he asked, "Do you think that is what God said?"

"God has never spoken audibly to me," I answered. "How do I know?"

"Why don't we just reschedule you for a week from Sunday," he said.

I put together a few color slides of what we had done in Brooklyn—and a brief message of what we wanted to do. Then I flew to Dallas.

After showing the pictures at the church and sharing the vision, Sister Hibbard said, "I believe God wants us to help this man buy that building in Brooklyn."

When they handed me the offering, I could hardly believe it. Ten thousand dollars—cash! No pledges. It was all right there. That was the largest offering in the history of our ministry. Now we had $10,098.16.

"Did God Tell You?"

THE WORD OF that meeting spread fast.

After I returned to New York I received a phone call on Wednesday from Clyde Causey, pastor of Glad Tidings Assembly of God in Sherman, Texas.

"We heard what happened at Sister Hibbard's church last Sunday. I wonder if there is any way you can be with us next Sunday."

"I can't do it," I told him. "I had to cancel on the pastor in Tyler to go to Dallas, and I've rescheduled him for this Sunday."

He said, "If you'll come to Sherman, we can really help your ministry."

"Did God tell you?" I asked.

He said, "No."

But I called the pastor in Tyler, and he understood. "Just come and be with us whenever you can."

That Saturday I flew once more to Dallas and drove up Highway 75 to Sherman, which is near the Oklahoma border. Again I showed my slides and shared the story. Then Pastor Causey asked his people to do their best to help us reach the children of New York.

The deacons were in the middle of counting the offering when the church treasurer called me into the office. She said, "We thought you'd like to see this."

On three large tables were piles of cash and checks that looked as if they belonged in Chase Manhattan Bank.

"The offering was eighteen thousand dollars. And here—take a look at this," the treasurer said, handing me an offering envelope. There was no address on it, just the writing of a man's name.

"Open it," she said.

I shook the contents into my hand. Thirty-seven cents and a piece of lint fell out.

Then she said, "This man is homeless. We thought you'd like to know that he put everything he had in his pocket in this offering." I'd never been around anything like this in my life.

In just eight days the Lord had provided twenty-eight thousand dollars—more than enough for the down payment on that building.

"Is It True?"

THE VISION FOR a mighty ministry to reach children was not only alive, but it was also burning brightly. The news that we had signed a contract on the old warehouse spread like a ghetto fire.

Young people who had worked with us before began to call. "Is it true? Is it really true?" said one.

Another begged to be appointed as a bus captain. He had seen Metro firsthand in his neighborhood. He wanted to be part of the love and compassion—the fun and the joy—that was in everything we did.

Even some of the older teens, who were on drugs, arranged for their younger brothers and sisters to be part of the program. "I don't want my little brother to turn out like me," said one young man.

Our workers and volunteers handed out thousands of flyers announcing the new Sunday school. We had long ago stopped renting buses in the area. All we had were a few well-used buses that had been parked much too long. One by one our mechanics brought them back to life.

We not only went back to visit homes in the old neighborhoods, but we also got out our maps and expanded the territory.

It was during that time that a little boy wearing no shoes or shirt asked a worker what he was doing. He said, "I'm inviting boys and girls to ride the bus to Sunday school to learn about Jesus."

The boy looked up at him and asked, "What's a Sunday school? Who's Jesus?"

The Traffic Jam

WHEN METRO CHURCH re-opened its doors that first weekend, the traffic jam on the corner of Evergreen and Grove was a sight. You could see the neighbors watching from every window. People stood motionless on the sidewalks as buses arrived from every direction.

More than twenty-four hundred children rode our Sunday school buses that first weekend.

In those days our staff consisted of just five dedicated people. In the cold of mid-winter, we were working hard to refurbish the dilapidated building. Every night we put a fifty-five-gallon metal drum on the cement floor in the middle of the auditorium of that old brick building. We'd find some scraps of wood to put in the drum and light a roaring fire. Then we would pull our sleeping bags close to the fire and get a little rest before starting work again the next day.

In those days we were nobodies. Not many cared if we stayed or went. I didn't get visitors or encouraging phone calls then. Now everybody calls. I know that's part of it. It's always a part of pioneering. But that's why I still won't send flowers to the funeral of someone I never sent flowers to when they were alive. If you care about somebody, tell them while you can. You may not get a second chance.

Once we got started again and people heard about the rebirth of our program, they began sending us things like carpets, chairs and gas heaters. We deeply appreciated the gifts, but they didn't pay the bills.

We also began to receive some hand-me-downs, sent from well-meaning people. One lady sent us a box of used tea bags— then she wanted a tax receipt for her donation.

We still receive more buses that are ready for the junkyard than you can imagine. Donors fail to realize it sometimes costs more to repair and fix the vehicle than it is worth to insure.

Many churches that pledge support for a ministry such as ours have an unrealistic idea of what is really needed on an urban mission field. Some people think that all we need are leftovers.

It reminds me of when I was a new Christian at the church in Florida. Every Tuesday the women's missionary council would meet to cut up bed sheets into strips, roll them up and send them to the missionaries in Africa. I could never quite figure out why they did this. All I could visualize was the natives receiving those strips and saying, "If we could just sew these together, they would make great sheets."

We thanked God for secondhand clothes, but we rejoiced when a work crew came for a couple of weeks in the summer and said, "We'll pound nails. We'll wash floors. We'll help hand out literature." Even so, the expenses we were facing required more than goods or services.

In Need of a Miracle

BECAUSE THE BUILDING was mortgaged, our budget had grown much larger than our income. Even flying out each Sunday to speak in churches didn't seem to be enough. We were seriously behind on our mortgage payments, and the debts were growing larger by the day. There were light bills, water bills, gas bills, insurance payments and more. Now that we owned a building, these things were new battles for us.

The guy we bought the building from saw people from all over the country coming to fix up the building, but our monthly financial support was still very small. Month after month we were getting more and more behind on the building payments. The owner saw his chance to get the building back and re-sell it for more now that so much work had already gone into it. He started the repossession procedures.

One day our bookkeeper said, "Bill, we are more than eighty-five thousand dollars in debt. What should we do? How are we going to pay the bills?"

Those who attended our Sunday school were certainly in no position to help. Our staff lived from week to week, often paid in salami sandwiches. We had very few regular, faithful supporters we could count on. We just had kids—more and more of them every week.

It got to the point where I hated to hear the phone ring. I knew it would be another creditor insisting on immediate payment.

We were facing another shutdown.

I thought, *How can I explain this to the lady in Sister Hibbard's church who gave part of her life's savings in that ten-thousand-dollar offering? How do I tell those wonderful people who supported us that I didn't know what I was doing?*

Then, out of the blue, Pastor Clyde Causey called from Sherman. He said, "Bill, you're not making it, are you?"

I said, "No. We're not."

He said, "We need to pay off the mortgage on that building, don't we?"

"Of course," I responded, "but I don't know how we're going to do it."

He said, "We are going to have a 'miracle Sunday.'"

"What in the world is a 'miracle Sunday?'" I wanted to know.

"I don't know, but we'll think of something," he said.

Several weeks later I had a phone call from Pastor Causey again. He said, "Bill, we need to make a movie of your work there. If people could just see what you are doing, I think they would support it."

44

"Do you know what it costs to make a film?" I asked him. "More than a thousand dollars a minute. Then you have to print copies. We can't afford it."

Bus to Brooklyn

SHORTLY AFTER THAT conversation I had a call from a former home missions director with whom we worked. He said, "We're making a film called *Mission America*. We'd like to include about a three-minute interview with you in the film. Greg Flessing and my son Bob are doing the work."

"Fine," I told him. "I'm here every Saturday to drive the bus; just let me know when." I did my interview for the film on the bus I drive while picking up the kids. And at the end of the day Greg came to me and said, "This is the last stop on our tour for this film project. We don't know you, but we believe in what you are trying to do here."

Then he said, "We don't have any money to give you, but we would be more than happy to make a film for you and not charge you anything. It will be our gift to this ministry. I just talked to the rest of the crew, and they said they would be willing to stick around tomorrow if you want us to. We've already got the technical equipment here." He finished by asking, "Could you use a film?"

"Could I use a film?" I repeated, stunned. Then I told them about my conversation with the pastor in Sherman, Texas.

The twenty-two-minute film was called *Bus to Brooklyn*. It was the story of what God had accomplished through this unusual ministry.

I contacted fifteen churches who had supported us from across the country and told them about our plan for a miracle Sunday.

They all said, "You can count on us. We'll help you."

We made fifteen copies of the film and arranged to have it shown in all these churches on the same Sunday, February 24, 1984.

On that one day the combined offering from those fifteen churches totaled $110,000. We had enough to pay off the entire

45

mortgage on the building and to purchase a tenement building near the church to provide housing for our staff.

As I surveyed what was happening in Bushwick, it was almost impossible to believe that not many months ago I had stood shivering on the hood of a secondhand bus and said, "Sorry, kids. It's over."

I was wrong. It was only the beginning.

Left: Saturday morning, buses line the streets while the sidewalks come alive. Sunday school goes into session!

Below: Workers, most of whom are products of the ministry, help lead the children to the auditorium in an orderly fashion. Metro's staff set an important example for the young ones.

CHAPTER FOUR

Blowing the Whistle

G IRLS?" I SHOUT into the mike. "Are you ready?"
They scream, "Yes!"
"Boys? Are you ready?"
Even louder screams.

Our little—but loud—percussion band sets the tempo, and we fill the room with singing. Last week we opened up with "He's Got the Whole World in His Hand." I like the second verse: "He's got New York City in His hand."

Next week we might kick off Sunday school with the chorus, "I Don't Know What You Came to Do, But I Came to Praise the Lord."

It's Saturday morning at 10:00 A.M., and the first of our three Sunday school sessions is underway. Metro Church has come a long way from what once was a filthy warehouse, but it's certainly not plush. That would be out of character with the neighborhood. It's clean, but it's certainly not elaborate.

The main auditorium looks more like an arena, with bleachers down the sides of two walls. Neatly lined rows of chairs pack the center. The long aisle down the middle is the dividing line—girls on one side and boys on the other. I learned a long time ago that when you deal with elementary and junior-high age kids, the fewer distractions the better.

Whose Child Is This?

We always begin by pledging allegiance to the American flag, followed by a pledge to the Christian flag.

By the Rules

WHAT HAPPENS NEXT is not hard to describe but is foundational for each of our classes. I always remind the children of the three basic rules. We put them up on the overhead projector. Those who have been coming for a while can recite them in their sleep.

"What's rule number one?" I ask.

"Stay in your seat," comes the reply.

Rule number two is "Don't sit on the red lines."

Our building should hold far fewer children than it does, but we pack every seat—and the bleachers too—with as many as the fire marshall will allow. We painted red lines around the seating sections to help keep order, to make room for the workers and for safety.

Then I tell them rule number three: "The whistle means quiet!"

"Let's practice that," I tell them as I blow the whistle.

It works. The noisy room is immediately silent.

Those who have observed Metro Sunday school are amazed at how quickly the students can change from being boisterous, hyperactive live wires to perfectly behaved little ladies and gentlemen.

If I want enthusiasm and excitement, all I have to do is ask, "Whose bus is the best bus?"

The kids literally scream out their bus numbers.

But if I want quiet, all I have to do is blow that whistle, and they are quiet. It's not a secret; it's just a process of education that kids can learn.

We have had public school administrators visit our sessions. They talk with me and say, "I don't know how you do it. We've had to give up having school assemblies because the students are uncontrollable."

I once asked a little boy on my bus route, "What is your teacher like at school?"

He said, "She just yells at us all day."

I asked him, "Well, what do the students do?"

"We just yell back at her," was the reply.

"All day long?" I wanted to know.

"That's right. All day."

Is it any wonder there are padlocks on the doors, police roaming the halls and teachers receiving either "combat neighborhood bonuses" or early retirement?

Trials and Errors

THE WAY WE conduct our Sunday school sessions is the result of thousands of trials and thousands of errors. But without question, what we do today works.

After a prayer and pledges to the American flag and the Christian flag, the service starts off with a bang. The songs are fast-paced with lots of action and excitement. From there the kids can't wait for the games to begin.

The game segment of the program is very important on many different levels. First, the kids will keep coming back if they enjoy themselves. Second, a lot of people have problems with discipline during the preaching time. If the kids are allowed to get rid of some of that energy they will be much more likely to sit still later on in the service. Third, we are able to review the previous week's lesson because the only way the children can come forward to play is if they know the answer to a question from last week's lesson.

Even during the message the contest between the boys and girls will be at work. We want the children to be quiet and pay attention, so we make it a contest: Who can behave the best? We give out points and prizes to the most well behaved. Then the children will want to pay attention.

Observers are often shocked when we announce that it is time to take an offering. But I believe that children need to establish a pattern of supporting the Lord's work through giving. The offering is symbolic. We have received everything from food stamps to subway tokens.

The priority of each class is the preaching time—a simple, one-concept lesson based on Scripture. The need for a personal relationship with the Lord and how it applies to them where they are is always presented.

Whose Child Is This?

Our target ages are children between five and twelve years of age. The nine-, ten- and eleven-year-old students make up the largest attendance.

If we are going to see a transformation in the coming generation, we've got to instill values while the children are young. We concentrate on what we do best—and believe that when those we train become parents, they will make a real difference.

When a young person reaches age fourteen or older, it is almost too late—the die has been cast. I believe in preventive medicine. It is a lot easier to make boys and girls than to repair men and women.

Knocking on Doors

IF THERE IS one key to the long-term success of our Sunday school it is the thousands of home visits that take place all week long—from the time students return home from school until the sun goes down. In the winter that doesn't give us much time.

Who makes the visits? The bus captains and their assistants. They have a roster of every child on their route, and they knock on each of those doors. In some neighborhoods one high-rise apartment may have enough children to fill an entire bus. In others the territory may be four blocks long and two blocks wide—but seldom larger than that.

Every week we print eye-catching flyers that tell what is going to happen at Sunday school that week. On any given day we are waiting outside elementary schools at dismissal to hand out the flyers to even more kids. If they are new on a route, we tell them to have their mothers phone the number on the flyer, and we'll assign them a bus number and tell them when it will come by to pick them up.

Several times each year we have special days.

Every year we give thousands of Christmas stockings to the children of the areas where we minister. They are sewn and stuffed by hundreds of women across the nation who believe in the work the Lord is doing at Metro.

The momentum continues to build with Operation Holiday Hope. Every child who goes to Sunday school receives a wrapped

Christmas present. For many this is the only gift they receive. We tell them that there is someone who really cares about them who bought the gift and wrapped it so they could have a special Christmas.

"White Castle Hamburgers" was the headline on a recent promotion. That's what the children would receive if they came that particular week. We are able to do such things because people stand behind us. In this case the hamburgers were paid for by a popular gospel music group from Ohio. They visited Metro Sunday school and were moved by what they saw.

I wish you could have been with me and a couple of my bus assistants one Friday afternoon at public school #145, on the corner of Central and Noll. We were waiting outside with the "White Castle" flyers when the doors flew open. There are no latches on the steel doors—you couldn't get inside if you tried. The security guards are inside, not out.

"Hey, show this to your mom," I said as I began handing out the flyers. "Are you going to be on the bus tomorrow?"

Within thirty seconds we were surrounded by children begging for the flyer explaining the hamburger day in Sunday school. Our regulars were giving us hugs and high fives.

They aren't given the White Castle burger until after Sunday school when they are on the bus. I am always surprised to see how many of the children don't eat it right away. They hop off the bus and hold it up for their moms and all the neighbors to see.

Tiffany, a little girl who rides one of our buses, told the bus pastor, "I can't wait to get home with my hamburger."

When asked why, she said, "I want to give half to my brother. He's never had a hamburger like this before. Isn't this great?"

Tiffany's little brother, Robert, was four. Nine months earlier he'd had an infection in his brain caused by the AIDS virus. Since that time he had not been able to speak or walk. His mother was an intravenous drug user and was in a government facility at Rikers Island. I believe if we are going to reclaim urban areas for Christ, we must be highly visible. The drug dealers, car thieves, drunks and prostitutes are visible. So are we.

53

Whose Child Is This?

We Are Family

THE RELATIONSHIPS THAT develop during those brief, but effective, visits in the home during the week carry the same weight—if not more—as the Sunday school program itself. Either one, however, is not successful without the other.

Many of our bus captains have been with us so long that they feel like part of the families they visit. Some of our volunteers were riding the buses themselves just a few years ago.

Our full-time staff are people who saw a need and are filling it. Much of their financial support comes from individuals and churches who designate regular gifts so they can continue this important work.

In my travels on weekends I am continually asked by enthusiastic pastors, "Can we send a bus load of our young people to help you next summer?" Or a parent might ask, "Do you have an internship program for my son or daughter? It would be such a great experience."

I wish I could say yes to all those kinds of requests. There are some cases where staff members want someone with a specific skill for short-term assistance, but for the most part, short-term doesn't work.

What we do is focused, time-intensive and at times dangerous. Our internship program accepts only applicants with strong pastoral references affirming that they quickly adapt to rules and have a passion to help and learn how to minister in the inner city. If you were in my shoes, you would understand that we simply cannot disrupt our mission to train people who work against us and not with us.

Do we need help? Desperately. The potential is so large and the need so great that we could have hundreds—even thousands—of workers. But they must be people who are committed to give their lives to such a ministry. That may mean five or ten or twenty years—or maybe a lifetime.

"What's Your Number?"

THE WORK NEVER ends.

Saturday morning at 6:00 A.M. the buses roll out to be cleaned and swept. At 8:45 the meeting for bus captains and assistants begins. That's when we hand out names and addresses of new kids who have called in for rides. We end the meeting by praying for God's protection and that the message of the day will make an impact.

By 9:00 A.M. the boys and girls begin to congregate on street corners or in front of their buildings. It doesn't make any difference whether it is raining or snowing. They are there with big smiles, just waiting to jump on the bus and say "hi" to one of their best friends, the bus captain.

An assistant is seated in the first row of the bus with a felt-tip pen to write the number of the bus on the child's hand so he or she won't get lost coming home.

These kids don't wait for the Sunday school to begin—they start singing while they are riding. Some mornings you can stand in front of Metro Church and hear the buses before you can even see them.

When the last amen has been spoken in the auditorium, the children head for their numbered buses. The captain counts heads, and they're off! For the bus captain the day is just beginning. After a short break and a quick sandwich, it's time to begin the route for the 1:00 P.M. meeting. It is repeated again for a 4:00 P.M. Sunday school.

People around the country are surprised to learn that I still visit the apartment of every child on my bus route—every week. It takes an absolute emergency to pry me away. Visitors are also surprised to see me actually driving the bus routes on Saturday.

For six years my personal visitation area was in the Bedford-Stuyvesant section of Brooklyn. But two girls who grew up with the program took over that bus route, and now my new assignment is in an extremely rough section of Bushwick.

Hardly a day goes by without a child running up to me, saying, "Here comes Yogi Bear." That was a life-size cartoon character we used in the early days of our Sunday school to get the kids' attention. People still call us the Yogi Bear Sunday school.

It would be easy for me to commute from a nice home in the suburbs and only show up in time to speak. That's what the leaders of many urban ministries do. But to me there is only one way to lead people—and that is by working shoulder to shoulder with them.

I like what Dr. C. M. Ward has said many times. Leaders must lead from the front. Even if you're getting run out of town, get out front and make everybody think it's a parade.

I am totally convinced that our acceptance in Bushwick and the growing number of ghettos where we minister is because we all live, eat and sleep in those neighborhoods. This is our home. These people are our neighbors.

When you stop to think about it, there is no logical reason why I should be treated as an equal by people living near our church. I am white—that's not too common. That will never change. But you can earn the right to be heard; it just takes more time than most folks are willing to put into it.

Why am I accepted? Because I climb the same filthy stairways the children do. Because I hug them whether they have on designer sneakers or no shoes at all. Whether they have lice in their hair or not. People respond to love and concern. They are tired of promises from people who disappear into the night. They want reality.

The Connection

OUR ENTIRE MINISTRY is based on relationships. It would be impossible to visit the same families week after week, month after month and year after year without developing an emotional connection. Commitment is important, but it is not enough to keep you in the ghetto in the dead of winter when it's ten below zero or in August when it is a hundred degrees and every junkie on the block is giving you a hard time. You stay out there because you honestly care about those kids.

How else can you find a staff member who will work with you all night trying to get a bus running to pick up kids for Sunday school? We couldn't pay people enough money to do it unless the burden was burning in their bones.

Most people would quit the moment a ten-year-old, first-time visitor said, "I'm going to kill you," because they made him be quiet in Sunday school. How do you deal with it? You take the time to work with the child because you know if you don't, someday he probably will kill someone.

Mother Teresa, the missionary legend from Calcutta, was once told, "You couldn't pay me to do what you do."

She calmly replied, "Me, neither."

The day you hear that Bill Wilson is living on Fifth Avenue in a penthouse overlooking Central Park or the suburbs of New Jersey is the day you know this ministry is history. God has not called me to minister to the Du Ponts or the Rockefellers.

The longer you live in our neighborhood the less important it is to impress outsiders. We have given up trying to beautify the buses or even putting fancy signs on the church. It is only an invitation for bullet holes.

We used to paint the buses with our church name. Now we just leave whatever happens to be painted on the side. They are too old and the engines will blow eventually anyway, so why waste the money? You can spend five hundred dollars on a paint job and suddenly discover the paint is worth more than the bus!

When people think of our ministry, they associate it with me because I travel the nation to fuel the fire. But there are no stars in Bushwick.

It Boils Down to Preparation

MUCH OF THE credit for the first-class presentation of the gospel through the Sunday school goes to Chris Blake. When I was just starting the ministry in Brooklyn, I was invited to speak at a church in Manassas, Virginia, just outside of Washington, D.C. Chris came to the meeting. I learned later that it was the first time he had darkened the door of a church. He was so overwhelmed with the service that he committed his life to the Lord and knew beyond any doubt that he would be working in the inner city.

After working with Chris on a few projects I invited him to join our staff, and he's been here ever since.

Each Wednesday those involved in the production of the Sunday school program have a two-hour planning meeting. Although Chris and I have prepared ahead of time the point we are going to be driving home, we feel it's important for everyone involved to have a part in the final lesson preparation. It is important to have a variety of lessons and ways to teach those lessons. But the one filter that all the ideas must pass through is simple: Is it powerful enough to change lives?

"What's the best way to illustrate it?" I may ask. "What props do we need? What more can we do visually?"

Before leaving the meeting every worker has his or her specific assignment. On Thursday and Friday all the materials are gathered and scripts are written for that week's Sunday school. Then on Friday night we have a run-through of every key element of the session.

I wish I could tell you that the first session on Saturday morning is perfect, but that's when we work out the kinks. By session number two it's as good as it is going to be.

So when the lessons are written in the KIDS' Church curriculum, everything has been thoroughly taught and tested. (See back pages for curriculum information.)

As a result of having a clear focus and a specific commitment, there have been some serendipitous side effects—valuable results that we weren't looking for. It is especially true in our ministry to teens and adults.

When the kids outgrow their interest in an elementary/junior high Sunday school, they still want to be part of Metro. Now there are Club L.I.F.E. meetings during the week—Bible study and recreation—for teens who got their start with us. More than a thousand are involved every week.

The Sunday school has also produced a vibrant adult congregation—parents who saw the impact of Christ on their children. Our adult church has grown with several thousand attending multiple services.

I doubt there's a congregation like it anywhere in America. Over 150 of the adults are HIV positive. The figure is probably twice that number, but those are the only ones we know about. What should we expect when the people accepting Christ come from a culture of drug addiction and sexual immorality?

We conduct three funerals for every wedding. And they're not dying of old age. The average age of the people we bury is twenty-five. The principal cause of death is AIDS, followed by drug-related violence.

There is never a time when you can relax. If you ever do, it's over. And you can never forget where you are. One of the reasons we keep such tight reigns on visitors is because they just don't get it. Things happen fast.

We had a visiting youth group helping wash buses, which is innocent enough. But teenagers being what they are, the water didn't always land on the bus. Some of the people on the street were inadvertently sprayed. In the suburbs that may be funny—even if it's annoying. But here in New York City something like that can get deadly. The bad feelings escalated.

Instead of spraying water back, the neighborhood kids threw bottles. The encounters didn't stop; all afternoon the unrest fermented. We knew trouble was brewing, but we didn't know how it would end. That night as I was parking the van, the neighborhood kids began shooting. I pulled into the schoolyard across the street from the church and stopped the van to run after them. As I opened the door and stepped out of the van, a bullet came through the driver's windshield in a direct line to where my head had been a few seconds earlier.

Chris Blake is a veteran of this sort of thing, too. Over the years he's been in the middle of several gunfights. One time he was out driving and stopped at a light. A bullet blasted through the window of the passenger side of the van and whizzed through the driver's side inches away from the bottom of his neck. Unknown to anyone but God, his wife, Karen, had been praying for his safety at that very time.

We keep saying that things happen fast. One staff member was walking to the office in front of the elementary public school. He caught sight of a car going unusually fast. The next thing he knew, he heard screeching tires and the familiar pop, pop of gunfire. He actually felt the vibration of the ricocheting bullets off the fence. It happened so fast, he couldn't even fall to the ground. Since the driver was also the shooter, the car was swerving. He was aiming at someone across the schoolyard and down the street. Fortunately neither our staff member nor the school kids were hit. They had just gone in to their classrooms from recess only minutes before the shooting. But nothing could shield them from hearing the volley of fire.

A casual survey of the staff revealed that fifteen staff members have been in the middle of gunfire at one time or another. Many of the incidents happened in front of our church or their apartments. Some gunfights occurred while staff members were out visiting in the projects.

We know that God protects us. But we also know we cannot be frail or foolish. If we're fainthearted, we won't get anything done. If we're foolish, we'll walk into situations in which God is not obligated to intervene.

Winning and Losing

I REMEMBER THE night one of our workers made a bad decision to smash a young man's radio because of his conduct. Some guys can only tolerate being called a particular type of mother for so long. The young man and a friend came back and blew up two of our buses.

When we make a decision to ask for police help, we had better count the cost. One of our workers will probably be making visits in the offenders' tenement building the following week.

We have to make a decision: The troublemakers have nothing to lose; we have everything to lose. It can wind up like a wild West movie—the last one standing wins. It's the law of the ghetto.

Once we were walking down the street and somebody dropped a two-by-four from the top of an apartment building, only missing me by inches.

A staff member's wife was attacked while she was driving one of our buses. Two men jumped out of a van and tried to take her away. They fled only after she managed to press a hand-held warning siren.

One staff couple came home to find their front door missing. The apartment had been totally ransacked. They never did find the door.

Like a Maze

BECAUSE OF THE size of our program, I am forced to spend much of my time dealing with issues totally unrelated to my mission in life. I've always said all I ever wanted to do was drive the bus; it's kind of a running joke among some of our staff. I wish it were that easy.

In New York you spend an enormous amount of time fighting the system. The bureaucracy is like a maze. It seems that it takes three permits to be eligible for the one you need.

Every day there are detours and delays.

"Why is McDonald's closed?" I ask a passerby.

"Somebody blew it up yesterday," he replies.

"Why can't we park here?"

"Because the police are over there," I am told.

There's another hurdle we face. The larger the ministry grows, the more pressure I have to be on the road raising funds. There was a time when I'd fly out on Saturday night, speak in two or three churches on Sunday, then fly back on Monday morning. Now I'm often gone for a week or two at a time, speaking at churches and conferences, meeting with folks in the United States and in countries all over the world. I do that fifty out of the fifty-two weeks a year; year in and year out. Fortunately, I have a dedicated staff who also believes "the need is the call." They keep it all running smoothly whether I'm there in person or out on the road.

Many churches and ministries have opened in the area since we have been here. But they have also closed. I sincerely believe you do more harm than good by starting something you don't plan to finish. Your actions shout: "Christianity doesn't work—not here."

People continually make promises they will never keep. They say, "We'll pray for you," which often means they don't want to get involved. When we were forced to shut down the Sunday school that second year, I made a pact with God: "If You'll allow me to open again, I'll never, never leave."

Saturday Sunday school overflows with children from New York's inner city.

CHAPTER FIVE

Don't Throw
Them Away

AMERICA HAS A problem it refuses to face. *Unless there is a revolution in the basic education of our children, the nation will crumble from within. Our demise will not come from an economic collapse, but from moral bankruptcy.*

It's already well on its way. What I deal with each day in Bushwick, the South Bronx and in Harlem is not an isolated social phenomenon that will become extinct. The exact same problems are invading "Everytown, U.S.A." like a plague.

To educators, pastors, politicians and parents, I say, "Wake up!" We can no longer ignore what is happening to our children. Why do we place a forty-thousand-dollar price tag on a new BMW and zero value on a child who fails to meet our standards? We can't afford to throw them away.

"Don't Touch"

EVERY WEEK I am in the dingy apartments of children who are as naturally gifted and talented as any young people you can name. Yet because of their environment and circumstances, an *X* has been written on their foreheads. It says to the world, "Don't touch. Don't teach. Don't encourage. You're wasting your time."

God has given some basic principles of how we are to care for those less fortunate than ourselves. Scripture says, "When you harvest your crops, don't reap the corners of your fields, and don't pick up stray grains of wheat from the ground. It is the same with your grape crop—don't strip every last piece of fruit from the vines, and don't pick up the grapes that fall to the ground. Leave them for the poor and for those traveling through, for I am Jehovah your God" (Lev. 19:9–10, TLB).

We may no longer live in small villages, but we still have a responsibility to our neighbors. In earlier times if someone's barn burned down or if they needed help, the entire community would come to their rescue.

But following World War II a combination of the economic boom and the automobile helped to create what we call suburbs. In the migration, however, the poor were left behind. What was the result? The needy, already separated because of position and race, had been separated geographically as well. They filled the empty shells of buildings that had been left behind, forming what is now known as the ghetto.

Next came the race riots of the 1960s. Huge government spending programs were thrown at the problems of the ghetto. But by the 1980s most Americans realized that federal efforts had been largely ineffective.

What we do have are deeply entrenched programs that dominate the lives of the poor. Supposedly those in need can turn for help to:

- The educational system.
- The welfare system.
- The criminal justice system.
- The housing authority.
- The food stamp program.
- The medical system.

And there are many more. What experience has proven is that no single approach can meet the needs of those in poverty. What is even more tragic is that the programs don't work well with each other. Yet those are the institutions with which we are forced to deal.

Don't Throw Them Away

Guarding the Turf

UNFORTUNATELY, THE BASIC problem that exists in society can also be found in the church. Most groups begin with noble objectives, but over time their goal is changed from "How can I help?" to "How can I stay in existence?"

You only have to pick up a newspaper to know that social agencies guard their "turf" jealously. They want their territory—their piece of the pie—protected. What a difference it would make if agencies decided to attack the problem by working together. What would happen if the clergy in a community decided to join forces to solve one pressing issue? Very seldom do ministers of the same denomination, let alone different denominations, work together.

My experience tells me that this is not going to happen. Even within denominations self-preservation and personal advancement have become the deciding factors of involvement. Instead of rejoicing that thousands of children are being exposed to positive messages, I have been told, "Don't send your buses near our church—that's where we work."

I would be thrilled beyond measure if one hundred churches in New York City started a program exactly like ours. Even then we would only be scratching the surface. Unfortunately, when most churches establish their budgets and priorities, children are usually last on the list.

"Easy Answers"

THE URBAN AREAS of America—Los Angeles, Miami, Boston, Detroit, to name a few—are experiencing cultural conflicts and racial hatred at an increasing and alarming pace.

How does a wound heal when the scab keeps being pulled off? That is what is happening in New York. Everyone is either looking for, or expecting to find, quick and easy answers to the inner-city problem.

During the riots between the blacks and the Hasidic Jews in the Crown Heights neighborhood of Brooklyn, Mayor David Dinkins was pelted with bottles and rocks and told by the crowd, "The mayor is not safe here."

If he was not safe with the two thousand police who were in the area to support him that day, who is safe?

Inside—Outside

PEOPLE CONTINUE TO ask, "Bill, why the violence? Why the killings?"

First you have to look at the fabric of the community. Every neighborhood has its unique identity and feeling. Whether you are talking about a square mile in Brooklyn or a single high rise in the Bronx, it is a closed neighborhood. It has its own "insider vs. outsider" thinking.

If you live within the well-defined boundaries, you are an insider. But if you're not an insider and it's nighttime, you had better be looking over your shoulder.

During the day, however, it is different. That is the time when the outsiders cross boundaries freely. A white in Harlem or an Hispanic in Bayside, Queens, or a black in Bensonhurst can move around without suspicion. But after the workday has ended, the people in those neighborhoods know who belongs there and who doesn't.

When the sun goes down, much of New York becomes suddenly divided into small towns like Springdale, Arkansas, or Winslow, Arizona. That is true regardless of race or cultural background. Outsiders represent the unknown and are immediately under scrutiny.

Unfortunately, the older teenagers become the guardians of the neighborhood. With nothing better to do than hang out on the corner, they try—no matter what the cost—to develop some kind of self-image. Their first attempt at getting recognition might be to spray paint their names on a wall. They may steal a pair of sneakers, just to prove they can do it. If they really want to display their manhood, they might demonstrate how they can keep outsiders out of their neighborhood.

In countless areas every block, every neighborhood and every barrio (as it is called in Los Angeles) become their own fortresses.

Each person does what is right in his own eyes. It is called "taking care of business."

What I have described is just one of the reasons that so many ministries come and go in the inner city. After tackling the problem day after day, a feeling of hopelessness sets in. That is why people have stopped painting over walls that are covered with graffiti. It seems so futile.

A few years ago I wondered, *Why do so few people speak up in the community when they see a wrong being done?*

They keep quiet because they have come to understand who is really in charge. It's not the police, not the government, not the educational system and not the churches. The streets are ruled by self-appointed neighborhood tough guys who enjoy being "hard rocks," as they are called.

The social system I have been describing breeds frustration, which manifests itself in hate, turf wars, murders and self-indulgences of all types.

Because there is no future, the people develop a take-it-now mentality. Today is all they have.

You may ask, "What about the public schools? Couldn't they make a difference?"

Classroom Crisis

I WISH I could tell you that America's finest teachers are begging to be assigned to schools who need them the most. But this is not happening. When *Time* or *Newsweek* features a teacher of the year who is motivating students in some impoverished area, you are reading about the exception, not the rule. I've spent countless hours talking with students, teachers, parents and administrators about what is happening in the classrooms of the inner city. My conclusion is that, for the most part, the elementary schools are providing free baby-sitting services under the guise of education. Some are nothing more than holding tanks to keep the kids off the streets. I know that sounds harsh, but our schools have almost given up on preparing underprivileged students for the real world.

In most cases the teachers don't want to be in urban schools. More than one has confided to me, "I'm here because the pay is a little better."

The more they make, the better housing they can afford—farther and farther away from the neighborhood. We have become a nation where everyone knows the cost of something, but no one can tell you the value of anything.

Recently I asked a group of about twenty of the kids on my bus route, "How many of you have had your teacher curse at you?" Almost every one of them raised their hand.

What is the teacher's side of the story? One instructor told me, "How would you like to spend day after day with these ignorant kids in an over-crowded facility that feels like a prison?"

We have yet to see what would happen if a group of professional educators decided to expose young people to a dynamic, lively, well-planned curriculum that would give students specific skills and self-esteem. What would happen if the public schools educated children with the same amount of time, effort and creativity we use to minister to children at Metro Sunday school? I know the public school system is much larger than our ministry, but the same principles can be applied to achieve the same positive results.

Americans are obsessed with choosing easy options that don't work rather than considering difficult solutions that do. Most sociologists have finally admitted that excellent role models and hard-hitting education for students—particularly under the age of fourteen—are the greatest hope of a turnaround in our schools. I've known it for a long time.

The Hunger Factor

WE ALSO NEED to take a close look at the health needs of our young people—not just in the ghetto, but across the land. A principal in a West Virginia coal mining town said, "One quarter of our kids are on the federal free-lunch program. But actually three quarters of them should be. So many of them are so embarrassed about their condition that they won't ask for help. They would rather hide their poverty."

Don't Throw Them Away

National statistics show that one out of every five children goes to school hungry. Kids who are hungry in America rarely die of starvation; instead they tend to suffer from chronic malnutrition—they're listless and tired, can't pay attention in school and miss more school because they get sick so easily.

I recall talking to the late Mark Buntain, the noted missionary to Calcutta. He said that when he first went to India, the people told him, "How can we listen to the gospel when our stomachs are empty?"

What Buntain told me is true. On more than one occasion we have had children faint in our Sunday school because they had not eaten for a few days.

What can we expect when many of the youngsters try to survive on a twenty-five-cent sugar-water drink and a twenty-five-cent bag of potato chips for the whole day? It's no wonder they get so excited over a hamburger.

During one Sunday school session we gave a cash prize to the child who could remember the most about the Bible story from the previous week. A staff member said that a little girl turned to her and said, "Oh, I sure wish I could win that money."

"Well, what would you do with it?" the worker asked. She expected her to say that she would buy a doll or a toy.

The girl looked up and said, "I'd buy some groceries for my mom."

It is impossible for us to feed the twenty thousand who come to Metro Church every week. But we have established a program to provide food and clothing for especially needy families.

It Doesn't Work

YOU'D THINK THAT after living for years in Bushwick I'd get used to it, but I don't. When you spend a month with no heat in the middle of January, you have to work at staying calm.

You may ask, "Who would turn off the heat?"

No one. It's the system—it just doesn't work. The infrastructure of New York City is so old that the water pipes are exploding, and the sewers are seeping into basements. Steam pipes and boilers just give out. There is not enough money to keep up with repairs.

On the Lower East Side of Manhattan, many buildings are exactly as they were when the first immigrants arrived at Ellis Island. There has been plenty of talk about rebuilding our cities from the inside out—constructing new high rises in the place of slums.

They tried it in the mid-sixties, but it was not very successful. The new buildings were often uninhabitable within two or three years—nothing but graffiti, garbage and grime. The siding fell off. The elevators broke and were never fixed—and even if they were you'd be taking your life in your hands to ride one.

People who visit us for the first time usually ask, "Why do these people stay? Why don't they leave the city for a fresh start in another state, such as Oklahoma or Oregon?"

When you grow up in poverty and figure out a way to survive, a move is out of the question. I've met young people living in Brooklyn who have never even been across the East River to Manhattan. How could you convince them to go to Memphis or Minneapolis?

Most people become a reflection of their environment because that is all they know and see. On Saturday morning we try to expand their vision. We try to give them some options for their future.

The inner city is in a cycle of constant change. Something goes up; something comes down. A business opens and then disappears. We visit children in a tenement, and the next week a new family is there. A month later they have moved on, too. Where do they go? Perhaps they crowd in with relatives—perhaps to a homeless shelter.

To understand what these people experience, a staff member and I lived for three days at Grand Central Station and slept in the subway corridors. I spent one night on the steps of the New York Public Library on Fifth Avenue—it was fifteen degrees. We tried to talk to these homeless people who became our friends.

Every person's story has a common thread. As one indigent told me, "I just couldn't face it anymore. I had to get out of the rat race." If they weren't alcoholics when they came to New York, they got that way fast.

Don't Throw Them Away

The inner-city dilemma was not dealt with when it surfaced in the 1950s and 1960s. Now it has spread to population centers across our land. I have become tired of reading the words of sociologists and Christian leaders who write about "another generation being lost to street violence." How many generations will we lose before we wake up?

An Oasis

ONE TIME I had an out-of-town visitor riding on my Saturday bus route. "Look at that!" he said, pointing to a particular street.

Right in the middle of a neighborhood with broken sidewalks, garbage-lined alleys and boarded-up storefronts, something was totally different. It was an area about one block long that was like an oasis in the desert. Every two-story housefront was neatly painted. There were bright flowers in pots on the steps. There was even a spot or two of freshly mowed, deep-green grass.

"How is that possible?" he asked.

"The answer is easy," I told him. "Those people own their own houses. They're just taking care of their investments."

One of these days the welfare agencies and rent subsidy programs are going to wake up. Instead of using taxpayers' money to prop up absentee landlord slums, they will start investing in people. It doesn't take a rocket scientist to figure out that the government could purchase entire buildings for less than they are paying in welfare subsidies. Many believe the tenements should be turned into condominiums and tenants should be given free title to the property. That would give them the pride of ownership they so desperately need, which would motivate them to take care of their property.

We will never transform people with the current system of throwing money at them—especially when there is little accountability for the recipients. You can't legislate values or morality, but you certainly can insist on honesty in how funds are being spent. In our neighborhood, children can easily go into the corner grocery store and buy beer or cigarettes with food stamps.

The present system doesn't produce self-motivation. Thousands of people have walked away from their jobs because they can't make enough to pay four or five hundred dollars a month to live in a run-down tenement. If they are without work they get a rent subsidy. If they work they get nothing. Welfare needs to be pro-rated so that people aren't penalized for entering the job market.

If we want to build self-reliance, government handouts are not the answer. We need to concentrate our efforts on changing the way people think. To me it begins with a change of heart.

Government agencies need to wake up to the fact that billions of dollars can be saved annually by tackling the problem before it happens. For example, it costs approximately five hundred dollars for six weeks of counseling for a teen on the prevention of pre-marital sex. It will take fifty thousand dollars of public assistance funds to support the child of an unwed mother for twenty years.

We should learn the lesson from public health. It costs around eight dollars for a measles shot. It costs more than five thousand dollars to cover hospitalization for a child with measles.

Our entire ministry is built on prevention. We want to reach them before the needle hits their arms and the bottle touches their lips.

The Commission

"I SUPPOSE YOU know you're fighting an unwinnable battle," said a member of the White House staff. That comment came when I was in Washington, D.C., attending my first meeting as a member of the National Commission on America's Urban Families. President Bush called for the panel as part of his State of the Union address in January 1992. In that speech he said, "It's time to determine what we can do to keep families together, strong and sound in urban America."

There were eight members present, including the mayor of Dallas and the mayor of Knoxville, Tennessee. I am the only member of the commission who actually lives in a ghetto. Governor John Ashcroft of Missouri, an outstanding Christian, is the chairman. In preparation for the event I was sent a detailed questionnaire and was interviewed at length. An attorney asked me, "Have you been arrested?"

"Of course. Any good preacher who's worth anything has been arrested," I said jokingly. But they still let my nomination go forward.

One of our tasks is to write a report in one year. A staff researcher called and said, "We've read some stories of things that have happened to you. Do you think you're going to be around for a year?" She was serious.

At the initial session I learned why the wheels of government turn so slowly. Our first task was to define the word *urban*. Five hours later we were ready for the next step.

While I have doubts that a commission can transform our blighted cities, it is reassuring to know that urban families are finally being placed on the government's agenda.

But in Brooklyn we don't have time to talk about the problem. The need for action is too urgent.

Cleaning the Street

OUR GOAL AT Metro Church is to see our territory reclaimed one block at a time. We want to see the drug dealers, prostitutes and muggers gone. That is happening through our neighborhood watch program. Here is how it works.

We locate the strongholds—that is, where there is a high density of children on a particular bus route. For example, between Irving and Knickerbocker we have twenty-five to thirty kids. Then we find out if the parents of those children are coming to our Sunday services. If so, we will establish a "care and prayer group" in that block. If not, we encourage them to be part of the group. Some might call it a home fellowship or a cell group. They meet for weekly Bible study, worship and prayer in the apartment of one of our members.

The care and prayer groups usually have about fifteen or twenty people crammed into two rooms and a kitchen. Some are sitting on the floor because there are not enough chairs.

A staff member who works with the program said, "Not every pusher and junkie is gone, but we've made some significant progress."

When caring people join forces, anything is possible. That's why we can say, "We're taking back the city—one block at a time."

A man in our church has a Bible study twice every day with nine people present every time—he and his eight children. His wife is a crack addict who is gone every night and most of the days. He raises the children alone.

They have no furniture and no rugs—just wall-to-wall mattresses. The pillows have no pillowcases. There are no sheets on the mattresses. The father sits there, with his back against the wall, having Bible study with his kids. They also pray that their mother will come in from the streets, and our staff is helping in that effort.

It is for such a family that Christ came into the world.

A Flicker of Light

THE FALLEN ARE human, too. The lowliest person still deserves our kindness, our courtesy and a handshake. There are people in our neighborhood who have tried to make trouble for our program in the past, but I try to show them compassion and love.

The prophet Isaiah was foretelling the life of Christ when he said, "A bruised reed shall he not break, and smoking flax shall he not quench . . ." (Matt. 12:20, KJV).

I have yet to meet the person who does not have within him a flicker of light or a glimmer of hope. Everyone has the potential for total transformation. "Come now, and let us reason together, saith the Lord: though your sins be as scarlet, they shall be as white as snow; though they be red like crimson, they shall be as wool" (Isa. 1:18, KJV).

There is an old hymn we used to sing by Fanny Crosby called "Rescue the Perishing." In that song are these words of hope: "Chords that are broken can vibrate once more."

I plead for the child nobody likes, the one nobody wants to be around. I plead for the teenage girl who is pregnant and not married. I plead for the young man who has fallen into sin. I plead for the mother who has five children by different fathers. Even if there is just a smoking flax, the Lord is not going to put out the fire. Anyone can be used of Him.

Don't Throw Them Away

Every child in America is a perfect patch just waiting to become part of the quilt God is making.

We can't afford to throw any of them away.

Bill Wilson and two neighborhood boys get ready to enjoy some good old food for the soul in Sidewalk Sunday School.

Along with food for the soul, these girls enjoy some good old food for the body!

CHAPTER SIX

"I Don't Want to Go Home"

T HE BUS WAS almost empty. The day's second session of Sunday school was over, and I was driving my load of kids back to their Bushwick tenement buildings. When I stopped in front of Jose's building, the little boy wouldn't get off the bus. He looked at the floor and sat motionless.

"Hurry up, Jose. It's time to go."

He didn't budge from the bus seat—very unusual, because he's usually the main talker and wanderer on the bus.

"Is something wrong?" I wanted to know as I pulled the bus to the side of the curb.

Jose didn't say a word, but I sensed the boy needed some special attention. His quietness was too abnormal.

"Would you like for me to walk you to the door?" I asked, taking him by the hand.

He nodded, and we began to climb the three flights of stairs to his apartment. When we reached his floor he began to squeeze my hand as if he didn't want to let go.

I sat down on the top step, and Jose threw his arms around my neck and said, "I don't want to go home."

"Why not?" I asked.

He pulled up his T-shirt, and I saw that the word "Jose" had been freshly carved into his stomach with a knife. I learned that the man his mother was living with had done it.

"I don't want to go in," he said as he began to cry. "I want to go home with you."

On that dismal stairway I realized that I did not come to New York's ghettos to reach ten thousand or even a hundred thousand children. I came for Jose. You see the masses. And you have to think in those terms. But the masses are made up of individuals.

Even though I made arrangements for Jose to go to Puerto Rico to live with his grandmother I can still see his face. He's one out of a thousand. But we were there for him when he needed us the most.

Dancing in the Street

"SLEAZY."

That's how everyone described Rowena when she brought her two little girls to Metro Church week after week. After they were safely inside, she would hang out on the stoop and mock the ministry.

Rowena was an attractive young lady, but her behavior was anything but beautiful. She wore suggestive clothing, made lewd comments to those who passed by, and if she heard music she would start dancing on the sidewalk or in the street.

When members of our staff would try to talk with her, she would either stare them down or begin to curse the church. "You Yogis can go straight to hell," she would say—referring to the Yogi Bear mascot we used at that time. There was obviously no place for the Lord in her life.

As a child Rowena had some church background but later turned her back on God. She was raised in an atmosphere of physical abuse. She had seen her mother battered, and she herself had been abused by the two men who fathered her children. She and her daughters were now living with her mother.

But there was another side to Rowena. She was an intelligent young lady who was a student at New York University, preparing to be a nurse. She also had a grandmother who knew the Lord and who continued to pray for her. Deep in her heart Rowena knew that if her two girls were to have a future, they belonged in the house of God.

One of the young men in our church was finally able to break through her defenses and strike up a conversation with her. Rowena said later, "I thought he was kind of cute," explaining why she even bothered to talk with him.

He ignored her outlandish behavior and didn't flirt with her. Instead he kept talking to her about his relationship with Jesus. Finally one Sunday she decided to accept his invitation to attend a service.

That morning I preached a message titled "Build Your Own Altar." I told the congregation, "Don't count on someone else's Christianity for your salvation. You look to Jesus."

The sermon was exactly what Rowena needed because she believed the church was full of hypocrites. With so many new converts it is easy to find people who have not totally given up their old lifestyles. The young lady used those people as proof that this "Jesus business" didn't work.

The next Sunday, to the surprise of many people, she returned. When the invitation for salvation was given, Rowena rushed to the altar and began to cry out to God.

Her heart was drastically transformed. The blasphemy was replaced by blessing. The scorn was replaced by salvation. What a turnaround! Suddenly the church became the focus of her life. She volunteered to help with the Sunday school—and eventually was given her own bus route.

At home, however, the tensions grew worse. Her mother became abusive and in one violent act of rage threw Rowena and the two girls out on the street. Her mother even refused to attend the graduation ceremonies at New York University where she graduated in the top 10 percent of her class—and was presented with scholarships for advanced studies.

Rowena and the girls have a bright future. She has an excellent job as a private-duty nurse and is enrolled in Bible courses to prepare for a life of ministry with her new husband, a fine Christian man from the ministry.

She told me recently, "I shudder to think where I might be if it were not for the church. You all were there all the time, but the main thing was you were there when I needed you."

"She's Coming!"

TIME AFTER TIME I have come face to face with situations that only the Lord can work out.

There have been many nights when my eyes have not been able to close. On those nights I can only stare at the ceiling, thinking about the tragic stories of families on my bus route. These people are "mine." I get so close to the children and their parents that their trials become my own. It drains you, but it has to be that way.

Because of the dangerous drug trafficking that was happening in one tenement building, a mother I knew well took her little one-year-old daughter and returned to San Juan, Puerto Rico. Her son stayed behind and moved in with some relatives. He continued to ride my bus to Sunday school every week.

Nearly two years later, on a Saturday morning, the little boy bounded through the door of my bus and shouted, "She's coming! She's coming! My mom is coming back next week."

He was going to be reunited with his mother and little sister. They would be a family again—even if that meant living in the squalor of a run-down tenement building.

A few days later I saw the little boy again, but this time he was crying.

"What's wrong?" I asked him.

The story that unfolded was not pleasant. When the mother returned to Bushwick, she had forgotten one of the fundamental rules of the neighborhood: Never allow your children to take food to bed with them.

One evening, earlier that week, the mom—not thinking—let her small daughter take a snack to bed. The woman left the building for only a short time, but by the time she returned tragedy had struck.

The child had fallen asleep with food on her mouth. A rat had crawled into the crib and had eaten away not only the food but the little girl's lower lip.

Immediately I went to the home and did my best to comfort the mother and her little daughter. She told me in her halting English, "I do not think anybody cared." The son asked why God had let this happen.

She didn't know what to do. They had no medical insurance, and the father had been gone for years. Sadly, her story is multiplied a hundred thousand times in New York. You try to give them an answer.

We were able to find emergency medical help for the little girl, but it seems that we can never do enough—and it never gets easier. What is sad is to realize that millions of people face tragedies just that traumatic every day, and there is nowhere for them to turn. Someone must be there to point them to the love of the Lord. There are problems only Christ can solve.

I'm only one person, dealing day after day and year after year with a few families that I have come to love and care about deeply. Every member of our staff has his or her own chronicle of the lives of those to whom he or she ministers.

But think of the millions who have no shoulder to cry on—who have no one who visits them every week. "Rescue the perishing, care for the dying." It sounds good, but it's going to take more than a few committed diehards to rescue a whole lot of anything.

Miguel's Prayers

RECENTLY, AFTER I spoke at a Christian education conference in Pennsylvania, a man asked me, "Bill, don't you ever feel like starting an orphanage or adopting some of these children?"

I immediately thought about Miguel, who accepted Christ as his Savior at the young age of eight. The boy had no idea how much that decision would impact the events of his life.

Within six months he lost both of his parents. In November his mother died of diabetes. Then, one week before Christmas, Miguel's father was sent to prison for murdering a prostitute.

Unfortunately, Miguel was placed in a foster home where the father was an alcoholic and the foster sister stole from his personal belongings to support her addiction to drugs.

As time went on I noticed Miguel hanging around the church day after day. It was as though he didn't want to leave.

"You sure like this place, don't you?" I said to him one afternoon.

"When I get bigger, I want to live right here and help in the Sunday school."

Eventually Miguel's prayers were heard. A young couple on our staff became the legal custodians of Miguel, and he became part of the team.

A Hug for Danny

HUNDREDS OF THE children we deal with are born into families where love has somehow been lost. That is the story of Danny.

One morning, when he was only three, Danny was sitting in his crib with his legs sticking out of the side slats. His mother, infuriated by his crying, jerked up the side of the crib, and both of his tiny legs were broken.

The physical abuse did not stop. Doctors say his mild case of cerebral palsy is the direct result of a severe blow to the head.

At the age of eleven Danny took matters into his own hands. He ran away from home and spent two days riding the subways. When he was exhausted he found his way back home. His mother was waiting for him with a two-by-four.

School officials noticed his bruises and immediately sent a social worker to the home. But his mother forced him to lie about his condition by threatening him with more beatings.

It was during this time in his life that a Metro staff worker knocked on the door of his apartment and invited him to ride the bus to Sunday school. She said, "Jesus loves you, and I love you, too!" And she gave him a big squeeze.

Danny was not used to hugs. He decided to come to Sunday school because "that lady talked about love, and I wanted some." He became a familiar face at church.

By the time he was thirteen Danny was asked to be an assistant to one of the bus workers. As they had done so many times before, his parents threatened to kick him out of the house. But Danny persisted. In fact, he brought his little sister to Sunday school, and she found Christ.

Today more than half of the boys in Danny's neighborhood are in jail or on crack. But Danny found the way out. He is working with the Sidewalk Sunday School staff and says, "My goal is to be involved in ministry full time."

Best of all, Danny is working hard to build a healthy relationship with his mother. "Jesus makes all the difference," he says.

For years I have heard Christians complain that "young people are so difficult to reach with the gospel." That may be true. But here is what I have discovered again and again: Young people are easily reached through a positive, loving relationship.

So often zealous workers are quick to tell someone that they need Jesus—and don't understand it when they are rebuffed. Instead, young people need to "see" Jesus through a demonstration of our love and concern.

Danny's life might have been lost forever if it hadn't been for a bus worker who gave him a hug, was in his home every week, listened to what he had to say and actually responded to it.

"Is It Worth It?"

THOSE WHO TAKE a close look at what is happening in Bushwick and the other ghetto areas of New York City realize that our staff is involved in much more than playing cute little games or presenting an hour of Sunday school. Over ten thousand children are visited personally in their homes every week. That's not as the Lord leads. That's not as the Spirit moves. It's every week. Rain, shine, snow or sick. Our motto is you don't call in sick; you crawl in sick. That is where the real ministry happens.

On those vital visits we observe the children closely to discern their nutrition, clothing and living conditions. When one of our workers spots a child at risk, we do everything within our power to provide immediate help. Churches and individuals across the nation give us food and clothing for urgent needs. Through our "Won by One" child sponsorship program, we have been able to brighten the futures of a growing number of children who are the victims of the inner-city cycle. We have done this by having an ever greater involvement in their lives with the help of individual sponsors from around the country.

Many stories could be written about the children of Metro Sunday school. They are not statistics in a government poverty report, but they are young people with names and faces that you cannot forget.

Gerald came to Sunday school week after week with a worried look on his face. He finally told his bus captain, "My older brother has not been home for many weeks. We don't know what has happened to him."

A few days later the worker learned that his brother was found on the street—dead from a drug overdose.

Cathy rode the bus every week, but on the weekly visits she would never invite her bus captain to come inside her apartment because she was ashamed of her mother. Then one day her bus captain went to visit Cathy and found her no longer there. She had been sent to live with relatives. Her mother had been arrested for operating a house of prostitution in their apartment.

Patrick's father is in jail for first-degree murder. Isabel's mother is in a mental institution because of addiction to drugs.

Kim has permanent scars on her forehead from the physical abuse she received at the age of five.

Tamara's brother is on a life-support system because of a bullet lodged in his spine.

Martha and Owen, a brother and sister, are wards of the state because their parents abandoned them.

And some still ask, "Is it worth it?"

A Different World

COMPARED TO THE number of Sunday schools nationwide, there are relatively few inner-city ministries. The explanation is easy: It is hard, sweaty, dirty work. Week after week our staff battles everything from rats to fatigue—from muggings to finding lice in our hair.

"I Don't Want to Go Home"

Without question, it is much easier to answer the call to be the Christian education director of a suburban church in Dallas or Duluth than to face the tension of the ghetto day after day.

Recently we had the use of a pickup truck, and it was often filled with young people on our Thursday and Friday afternoon visitation routes. One day a man threw a cinder block from the top of an apartment building and smashed the fender of the pickup, missing one of my bus workers by less than a foot. It could easily have killed her.

That's not what the average church worker faces. But we do.

Gang involvement is on the rise in New York. Now along with the Asian gangs in Chinatown, which deal in extortion and drugs, kids and staff have to deal with the threats of gangs. Kids in Brooklyn and the Bronx don't trust anybody—with the rise in gangs, fear is added to that distrust.

One young man told me, "I don't trust girls, guys or anybody. Someday they will all stab you in the back."

The troubled youth in Brooklyn, the South Bronx, Harlem and other communities hang out together but don't seem to run in packs or organized groups per se.

Every neighborhood where we minister has a unique culture that must be understood. For example, we present a weekly Sidewalk Sunday School in a Chinese community—and this is the most evangelism the area has ever experienced. There are about three hundred in attendance. But it is a total contrast from our other points of ministry because so many of the adults are present with their children. The Chinese maintain an extremely strong family unit. Our flyers are printed in Chinese and our main workers are from the China Inland Mission organization.

Absorbed by the Culture

EVERY YEAR WE sponsor a national workshop for inner-city ministers in Phoenix, and I recently shared one of my great concerns about living and working in the ghettos. I told them, "If you are not careful, you will become the very thing you go to change."

Without question, it is imperative that you relate to the people to whom you minister. You spend time in their homes. You share in their daily struggle for survival. But I have seen dedicated, concerned workers lose their vision because they adopt the mind-set of the ghetto culture that says, "Nobody cares. I'm not going to make it. The future is hopeless."

It would be foolish for me to cultivate my passion and zeal for ministry without continually asking God to restore my vision and renew my spirit. Otherwise it would be impossible to provide inspiration for our staff and raise the funds necessary to continue this work.

There are some days I wonder if I will ever get used to living in such a "foreign" environment. I'll always be white. To many I'll always be an outsider no matter how long I live here.

One evening a family I was visiting invited me to stay for supper. Of course, I accepted. I could smell something cooking in the kitchen, and I thought, *It's either rice and beans, or beans and rice!* This evening it was even better: pork chops and mashed potatoes.

Furnishings in the home were sparse. The children were sitting on plastic milk crates. Then, halfway through the meal, I noticed two antennae coming out of the mashed potatoes. A large cockroach walked right out of the bowl and crawled down the edge of the table.

Someone said, "Don't worry, preacher; he doesn't eat much."

The conversation continued, and nobody seemed to pay the slightest bit of attention to our extra guest. Then the mother handed me the bowl and said, "Here, pastor, have some more."

I said, "You know, I really am full."

A writer for *Guideposts* magazine called me while she was preparing an article on Metro Church to accompany the Church of the Year award. She asked, "How much longer can you do what you do?" I don't have cute little answers for those kinds of questions anymore. I used to have an answer for everything. Now it's an effort to just listen to the question.

Do I ever get discouraged? Yes. Do I sometimes feel overwhelmed? Yes. But then something will happen that brings it back into perspective. When *Parade* magazine published a feature story about

Metro Church, the wife of a famous athlete sent me a hand-written note that said, "We lost our precious son to drugs. Thank you for the wonderful help you are giving these children."

The New Generation

ONE FRIDAY, AFTER I finished another afternoon of climbing the stairs to visit the apartments of every child on my bus route, I returned to my office totally beat. The little voice inside was saying, "I'm really tired." Everyone knows my schedule, and so it's a running staff joke that nobody ever says they're tired around me.

As I opened the door to our administration building and began to walk through the lobby, I suddenly stopped and looked around the room. I saw the same helpers, assistants and volunteers whom I work with week after week, but at that moment I realized who they were.

In that room were teens and young adults who had literally grown up in our Sunday school program. I could still remember them as small children. Now they were taking on responsibilities in a Sunday school program that had changed their lives. They were becoming leaders in their own right—reaching out to a new generation.

At one office desk was Maria, completing a report on her visitation. When she was only seven or eight, she attended the first Sunday school we opened in Bushwick. Now she is graduating from high school and has been accepted to Kingsborough College.

In my travels I continually meet sharp, intelligent young people in every part of America. Maria is no different. I would put her up against any suburban teen in Minneapolis or Memphis. But it would be almost impossible for most people to comprehend what her life has been like at home—just down the street from Metro Church.

Maria's mother has a drinking problem and no time for the Lord. Her father has been arrested for dealing drugs—I see him week after week hanging out with the wrong crowd on the street corners of Bushwick.

Whose Child Is This?

Some young people would run away from such circumstances, but not Maria. "Why should I go anywhere else?" she told me recently. "There's no place that's cared about me as much as Metro. You are like my father."

She is totally involved in every aspect of the ministry—Sidewalk Sunday School, teaching classes for small children, office work, door-to-door visitation and assisting the bus workers.

Like so many others, Maria has no plans to leave Bushwick. "I have two younger sisters at home. Who would look after them?" she explained.

That afternoon, I saw Maria and the other young people whose lives have been impacted by what has happened in Bushwick. *Should I slow down?* I asked myself. *But how can I?*

Recently I read through stacks of handwritten notes from the children about why they like Metro Sunday school. Here's what some of them said.

- Makisha wrote, "My bus driver's name is Karen. Every time we come in the bus she gives us a kiss. She loves us all. I like Sunday school because the teachers tell us about God and tell us not to steal or put our lives into sin."

- Justin said, "I like Sunday school because it has games and stuff and talks about God. I like the people in Sunday school. I like the bus driver that cares about us."

- Eddie wrote, "Every Saturday I get up real early and wait for my bus. We sing real loud when we ride. That is my happy time one day every week. Thank you."

- LeMar is only eight. He said, "Sunday school has done a lot for me. It has taught me how to pray to Jesus. It has also taught me how to stay away from sin. Sunday school has also helped members of my family. My mother and grandmother both pray every day now."

"I Don't Want to Go Home"

"Happy Birthday"

A FEW WEEKS ago Chris Blake, our Sunday school director, brought in an old plastic bag that was given to him by one of the younger kids on his bus route. The boy told Chris, "Here, I want you to give this to someone who is homeless."

The bag was filled with an odd assortment of well-worn clothes and tattered toys he had collected. "If they don't have a home, they probably don't have enough to wear. And their kids probably need some things to play with."

What impressed Chris was the fact that this little boy was perhaps the poorest child on his entire bus route.

This is the kind of child who makes our journey such a joy.

On my birthday a little boy on my bus route gave me a card. It was a used card. The corners were dog-eared, and it was bent and smudged. Someone else's name had been erased and mine put in its place. Here's what it said on the front:

Happy Birthday!
You Are Three!

But on the inside he had scribbled the words, "Pastor Bill, I love you."

Birthday presents don't get any better than that.

Metro Ministries founder Bill Wilson with some neighborhood kids.

CHAPTER SEVEN

The Power of Personal Visitation

T HE STORIES YOU have just read are very personal and all too real. But these kinds of relationships don't just happen. They are cultivated by a very strong and consistent presence in these kids' lives over a long period of time. This is accomplished primarily by personal visitation, which has literally become the foundation for this entire ministry. I don't want to sound like a broken record, but it's really true.

During the Korean War a young American couple got engaged. The military draft interrupted their plans, and the future husband was called into active duty in the Army. The young bride-to-be was heartbroken when her fiancé was shipped overseas. In their tearful farewell, the young soldier promised that he would write her daily—even if it was only a postcard—telling her how much he loved her. As soon as he returned to the States, he promised, they would be married.

To prove his intentions, he bought 365 postcards, put stamps on them and bought a special carrying case just to take them overseas. He never missed a day. With precise regularity, the postcards came to the girl's home daily. Each card carried a message of tender love and endearment.

At the end of the year the young woman married—not the soldier, but the postman.

Whose Child Is This?

It was not the postcards that impressed her. It was the personal visitation.

The Secret to High Attendance

OUR SUNDAY SCHOOL is averaging well over 20,000 in weekly attendance, and that's only the students twelve years of age and under. What is the reason for the high numbers? Our staff is composed of more than one hundred full-time people and more than 350 volunteers who make *more than 20,000 personal visits to these kids every week.*

When I repeat these figures to pastors, they either think I'm lying or we're some kind of supermen. Neither is correct. I simply believe the secret to high attendance in any church program is personal visitation, and I'm willing to do what it takes to get the job done.

I'm sure the lack of visitation programs in most churches is not without justifiable reasoning. As modern-day evangelicals, we can justify most anything we want to if we work at it long enough. But the fact remains that the New Testament church went daily from house to house. I still believe that we must go out and compel folks to come in. That word *compel* means to provide a way—any way.

Unless we are on the field on a perpetual basis, I do not believe we can expect to build the kind of relationships it takes in today's world to influence a generation for Christ. And that's precisely what we are trying to do in New York City.

Why does a consistent visitation program work?

1. *Personal visitation places people (both paid and volunteer) in someone else's world.*

Because of the nature and composition of our society, few average, middle-class Christians make a concerted effort to enter the world of a child, teenager or adult other than in their own families. It's a lot easier to go month after month locked in our own worlds, our lives revolving around family, job, free time and personal comfort. When we step out of that comfort zone and go into someone else's world—a world that may be foreign—it can and will be uncomfortable.

Sometimes breaking out of the comfort zone puts us into an unfamiliar social stratum. For a number of reasons, it is easier to associate with the people with whom we feel comfortable. That's why most people have friends who are just like them. The sad part is that we begin to think everyone is just like us—when nothing could be further from the truth.

Getting into the reality—as we do in New York every week—of ghetto families with problems too mind-boggling to describe forces us to be real. It forces us to face issues and challenges that most Christians have never had to face before.

It's easy to believe a theology that is never challenged. But it's better—so much better—to believe a theology that has been challenged and has won every test.

In *The Velveteen Rabbit,* a children's story by Margery Williams, an old skin horse that had been in the toy box for many years talks to a newcomer stuffed rabbit about being real.

"What is real?" asks the rabbit one day. "Does it mean having things that buzz inside you and a stick-out handle?"

"Real isn't how you are made," replies the old horse. "It's a thing that happens to you. You see, when a child loves you for a long, long time, not just to play with, but really loves you, then you become real. It does not happen all at once. It usually takes a long time. By the time you are real, most of your hair has been loved off, your eyes drop out, you get loose in the joints and very shabby. But these things don't really matter at all, because once you are real you can't be ugly except to the people who don't understand."

That conversation, as fictitious as it might be, actually reflects the reality being sought by folks today. People down the street, up the block, in the suburbs and in the ghettos are all looking for someone who is real. They don't need someone who pretends to have all of the answers; they just need someone who is willing to be vulnerable enough to come and place themselves in someone else's world at the risk of being hurt—mentally, physically or emotionally. When that is done on a consistent basis, something happens to both the giver and the receiver.

2. *Personal visitation provides a person-to-person relationship.*

In the average church the actual time of ministry is extremely limited according to the schedule of the week. One of the beauties of the cell-group concept is that it allows closer interaction with folks outside of a large congregational setting. Personal visitation does the same thing.

Like all the staff members in our ministry, I drive a bus and pick up kids for our Sunday school. Each Friday I spend several hours visiting the kids who live on my bus route. The kids who ride my bus eagerly look forward to my coming around. It's the highlight of their week—and the highlight of our ministry.

Yes, it is important that I prepare the lesson that I teach. Yes, the content of that lesson is important. Yes, the organization of the entire outreach is crucial. But again, if people don't like me, they won't listen to me.

That's one of the most difficult things for so many Christian leaders to understand. I'm able to pack 120 ghetto kids into a sixty-six-passenger bus and not only remain sane but prevent bloodshed, because these kids know me and like me. So they listen to me.

I understand what's happening in the lives of the kids on my bus route. I'm in their homes every week. I know their moms. (Few have dads.) I know the struggles they are going through in school. I know the struggles their moms are going through. For many of these kids I have become the only father they know. Every Father's Day I get cards saying, "I wish you were my dad." The other workers in our ministry experience this as well. Such relationships would not be built if it were not for the person-to-person contact we have during the week.

3. *Personal visitation prevents alienation.*

The bus route I drive and visit weekly is in the Bushwick section of Brooklyn. Except for the cops who now patrol in threes, I'm the only white person on the street. On several occasions I have been beaten and stabbed. I'm often threatened. Gangs have tried to pull me out of the bus. Staff members have left because of psychological problems created by living here.

It would be easy for me to say, "I think I'll let someone else do this," or "I don't feel led," or "This must not be the will of God for me." But if I take that approach, I will become what so many other pastors, unfortunately, are—pencil-sharpening, paper-pushing administrators, so alienated from the people that they really think they are ministering by sitting in an office, living in the suburbs and writing books on evangelism.

That's why everyone on our staff has a bus route. We all visit. We all run the risks. We do it because everything rises and falls on leadership. I cannot expect anyone in this ministry to do anything that I'm not willing to do myself. Once we allow ourselves to become alienated from the people we have come to minister to, we lose our effectiveness. It's easy to teach and preach visitation and soulwinning from the pulpit; it's another thing to be out there leading the way.

4. *Personal visitation prepares personalities.*

I have watched many kids in our Sunday school grow up and start their own personal visitation programs. They know the value. They are not afraid to go out. They are not wondering what other people are going to say about them. As a result of visiting, many of these kids are now going into full-time ministry. You see, their personalities were prepared for the gentle tugging of the Holy Spirit by being out on the field on a regular basis, learning to give back what someone had given them.

5. *Personal visitation promotes productivity.*

I attend many Christian conferences. Constantly, I hear leaders loathe laziness on the part of church members. Yet those same leaders fail to see that personal visitation produces productivity. I have heard it said many times: If you brag on Cadillacs, you will get Cadillacs. If you brag on good Sunday school teachers, you will get good Sunday school teachers. If you brag on good soulwinners and a good visitation program, that is what you will get.

Do not delegate personal visitation to a committee. A committee is "the unfit, appointed by the unwilling, to do the unnecessary." Rather, take a couple of people who have visitation and soulwinning burning in their bones, give them some direction and turn them loose to visit weekly. Then talk about their productivity in the bulletin and from the platform. Brag on them. There is no telling what may happen to your church.

For five years I worked for Tommy Barnett, now pastor of Phoenix First Assembly of God, who was then in Davenport, Iowa. Tommy, who is beyond a shadow of doubt the greatest soulwinner and motivator in this generation, said something that has stuck with me through the years: "Your week revolves around your soulwinning and visitation time; your soulwinning and visitation time does not revolve around your week."

I've built on that. The secret is to set a specific time each week to go out and visit, whether you're visiting your Sunday school class, youth group, bus route or part of the adult congregation. Set that time aside to build relationships with the people—and don't let anything squeeze the time out. It just boils down to discipline and priority. Make sure that your folks not only will be in services or classes the coming weekend, but that their needs are being met. Be prepared to win them to the Lord in their own homes.

Several years ago a high-profile denominational leader came to New York City and wanted to see me. His only schedule opening was at 3 P.M. on Friday—in Manhattan. I had to tell him I could not make it because that was the time I visited the kids on my bus route. I'm glad he understood. In fact, he actually congratulated me on my commitment. I knew I was running the risk of offending one of the bigwigs—but that's the kind of commitment it takes to get the job done.

6. *Personal visitation projects an image.*

Every ministry today projects a certain image in its community. The question is, What kind?

Everyone in our section of New York knows who we are. Our building is certainly not the largest building in the area. It doesn't even look like a church. It's an old warehouse. We do not have a

TV or radio program. We do not have billboards all over town.

So how does everybody know about us? Simple. We have projected an image through our visitation program of being out on the street every week on every block throughout our neighborhoods. On any given day you can see our workers, Sunday school fliers in hand, going door to door, standing in front of elementary schools and on street corners, hanging out at parks and playgrounds, visiting with the kids on our roll sheets. Our personal visitation program has become almost an institution in the parts of New York City where we work.

We want to project an image of caring—and we are doing it.

As these young kids grow up and advance through the Sunday school into the pre-teen and teen departments, and then into the adult areas, my prayer and goal is that they will see in those of us who minister the vision that helped win them to the Lord and the burden that keeps us motivated. Seeing and being around love in action perpetuates that fire in others.

Back in the days of the Old West, the only way to keep the wolves away at night was to keep the campfire ablaze. We have seen the visitation program in our Sunday school provide the fire that has kept the wolves from devouring tens of thousands of kids. And now this same concept is spreading to major cities across America and around the world.

One Young Boy

EDWARD KIMBALL, A shoe clerk and a Sunday school teacher in Chicago, loved boys. He spent hours of his free time visiting the young street urchins in Chicago's inner city, trying to win them for Christ. Through him, a young boy named D. L. Moody got saved in 1858. Moody grew up to be a preacher.

In 1879 Moody won to the Lord a young man by the name of F. B. Meyer, who also grew up to be a preacher. An avid enthusiast of personal visitation, Meyer won a young man by the name of J. W. Chapman to Christ. Chapman, in turn, grew up to be a preacher and brought the message of Christ to a baseball player named Billy Sunday. As an athlete/evangelist, Sunday held a revival in Charlotte,

Whose Child Is This?

North Carolina, that was so successful that another evangelist by the name of Mordecai Hamm was invited to Charlotte to preach. It was while Hamm was preaching that a teenager named Billy Graham gave his life to Jesus.

It all started with the winning of a child to Jesus.

We may not all be a D. L. Moody, Billy Sunday or Billy Graham, but we can all be instrumental in beginning that process in the life of someone who will be.

I am not what people would consider an extremely gifted person, but I can go out every Friday and visit dirty kids sitting on the street corner that look just as I did when I was their age. Somebody came and visited me, and that's why I am where I am today. I'm not a Rhodes scholar; I don't have a lot of degrees behind my name. But I care, and you can care, and we can both take that burden into the streets.

We all want a personal visitation from the Lord. So often it comes through personal visitation for the Lord.

Right: Bill teaches with intensity while...

Below: the kids give him their full attention.

CHAPTER EIGHT

Fighting the Giants

"WE ARE GOING to have to take your eye out," the doctor in Dallas told me. "Our plan is to remove the blood clot surgically, then put your eye back in."

That was not the news I wanted to hear.

Three months earlier I was jumped from behind by two men in a robbery attempt near DeKalb Avenue in Brooklyn. I never saw it coming. They smashed my face with a brick. It fractured my cheekbone and broke a front tooth. But much more serious was the blood clot behind my right eye.

I had become totally blind in that eye and was forced to wear a patch. I had to continue to drive my bus route, make home visits and travel, raising funds every weekend. There was no one available to take my place at that time.

When two businessmen from Texas learned that I had no health insurance, they paid for me to see a Christian eye specialist in Dallas—an outstanding physician.

The initial goal was to dissolve the blood clot with saline treatments, but this was not working. Surgery seemed to be the only option. "We can never guarantee 100 percent success with such an operation, but I don't see any other alternative," the surgeon explained.

I don't mind telling you that I was scared. The date was set for the operation, and the businessmen sent me a prepaid ticket to Dallas. I was to fly from La Guardia Airport on Monday morning.

What nobody knew was that I also purchased an airplane ticket. It was my plan that when they dropped me off at the airport, I would use my own flight coupon—and the destination was not Dallas.

I didn't breathe a word to anyone. On Monday morning I would board the other plane and be gone. As far as I was concerned, I was never coming back. It was over. That's not a great testimony, and I know that, but that's where I was. I was done.

The morning of my planned departure, as the first rays of sunlight came through my window, I looked up at the ceiling and was shocked at what had happened. I could see perfectly—out of both of my eyes.

I canceled my flights and called the surgeon in Texas with the good news. "I'm healed," I told her. "There's no need for an operation."

Nobody had laid hands on me the night before. I hadn't been anointed with oil. My faith had become so weak, and I was so fearful that I wanted to run away. But that's where God stepped in. His strength was greater than mine. I can do a lot of things, but I can't heal myself.

More than once in my life I have reached that point where everything looks hopeless—where the problems are far beyond my ability to solve. In those moments I have seen God take complete charge of the situation. It may come down to the wire, but if you hold on, God comes! I don't understand it all. I just know that's how it works.

Taunted by a Champion

THE STORY OF David and Goliath has held some great truths for me personally. Most of us know the particulars of the story but might not be able to make the application. Many have made this story some sort of a miracle, but there were basic principles involved that once understood and applied can totally change the way we deal with battles.

Goliath, a champion warrior among the Philistines from Gath, was looking for a showdown with Israel. He was more than nine feet tall.

> He had a bronze helmet on his head, and he was armed with a coat of mail, and the weight of the coat was five thousand shekels of bronze. And he had bronze armor on his legs and a bronze javelin between his shoulders. Now the staff of his spear was like a weaver's beam, and his iron spearhead weighed six hundred shekels; and a shield-bearer went before him.
>
> —1 SAMUEL 17:5–7

Scripture tells us that he stood and cried out to the armies of Israel:

> Why have you come out to line up for battle? Am I not a Philistine, and you the servants of Saul? Choose a man for yourselves, and let him come down to me. If he is able to fight with me and kill me, then we will be your servants. But if I prevail against him and kill him, then you shall be our servants and serve us.
>
> —1 SAMUEL 17:8–9

One day a young boy who was tending sheep was asked by his father to take some roasted grain, some cheese and ten loaves of bread to the Israeli army camp. The young man's name was David. When he arrived he presented his gifts and immediately headed for the front lines to find his brothers. There he heard Goliath's challenge.

David asked the soldiers around him, "Who is this uncircumcised Philistine, that he should defy the armies of the living God?" (1 Sam. 17:26).

His oldest brother scolded him for such talk. "Why did you come down here? And with whom have you left those few sheep in the wilderness? I know your pride and the insolence of your heart, for you have come down to see the battle" (v. 28).

David continued to ask the same questions, and it wasn't long before King Saul sent for him. The young shepherd boy told Saul,

Whose Child Is This?

"Let no man's heart fail because of him; your servant will go and fight with this Philistine" (v. 32).

Saul said to David, "You are not able to go against this Philistine to fight with him; for you are a youth, and he a man of war from his youth" (v. 33).

Lions and Bears

IN THE NATURAL it appeared to be an unwinnable battle. So how do we win an unwinnable battle? What do you do when everything appears to be impossible?

The experience of David gives us the answer. All of his young life was spent tending sheep, hours and hours each day, just staring at sheep. Do you know what sheepherders do? Practically nothing. They sit on a hillside with the sheep for days—even months—with little to occupy their time.

It was there that little David learned to play the harp and to use a slingshot. In those quiet times he also learned to communicate with God.

When is the last time you spent time alone with the Lord?

Over the years, especially since living in New York, I have spent many lonely nights in a hotel room just looking out the window all night long. As difficult as the past few years have been, I feel closer to the Lord than I ever have because of the time I have been forced to be alone—thinking, praying and reading God's Word.

Winning an unwinnable battle requires that we be nurtured in solitude. I'd like to tell you there is an easier way, but there isn't. If you want to win a battle, you first need to get alone with God. It's not easy. If anybody knows that, it's me. But it has to be.

David's faith was not only nurtured in solitude, but it was also strengthened in conflict. He knew what the Lord had done for him in the past, and he was more than ready to face the giant.

Saul asked him, "What qualifies you to go out and fight? You're a nobody." Remember what David said.

"I fought a bear once, and I beat him. I fought a lion once, and I beat him, too." As far as David could see, this giant was just another fight (vv. 34–36).

This whole story was just not as big a miracle as we sometimes make it out to be. You see, most of us hate the battles. Me too. But if you run from one, you just keep running. Then when the giant of your life comes—and it will—you're going to go under. You won't make it. You have no battle experience. You have nothing to draw from.

The lions and the bears in my life have come in many forms: rejection, sickness, heartbreak, tragedy—you name it. But walking through such trials is how we get our battle experience.

God doesn't give you strength for the battle. He gives you strength *from* the battle. We want it the other way around. It just doesn't work that way.

Don't run from the battles. Stand there and square off. There really isn't anything that can be thrown at me anymore that can destroy me. I've fought a few lions and bears, and a giant too. And by God's grace I won.

The Final Test of Faith

WHEN DAVID STEPPED on the battlefield, he had nowhere to hide. He was just one small shepherd challenging a monster. But when David spoke, his words were not of his weakness but of God's strength. He said to the Philistine, "You come to me with a sword, with a spear, and with a javelin. But I come to you in the name of the LORD of hosts, the God of the armies of Israel, whom you have defied" (v. 45).

We all know how the dramatic story ends. David reached into his pouch and took out a stone.

This was David's final test of faith. His faith had been nurtured in solitude and strengthened in conflict, but it was proven in hopelessness.

David knew his answer was not in his slingshot. If he had been certain of his ability to use it, he would have taken only one stone instead of five. The young shepherd had no illusions regarding his own power. He was completely reliant on the Almighty.

When the situation is hopeless, there is only one place to turn. As the psalmist wrote: "I will say of the Lord, 'He is my refuge and my fortress; my God, in Him I will trust'" (Ps. 91:2). Even when it looks like it's over, it ain't over till it's over.

Where Was the Guidebook?

I'VE SPENT CONSIDERABLE time over the years giving advice. Requests continue to cross my desk almost every day to give a how-to seminar on everything from building the actual Sunday school program to confronting drugs and crime in the inner city.

Recently I came to the conclusion that if you know why you are doing something, you'll figure out how to do it by yourself. Necessity is still the mother of invention.

Experience has proven that if you have a burning passion to reach an objective, it is rare that you need a guidebook to show you the way.

As a teenager in St. Petersburg I launched a ministry that was essentially what I am still doing today. There were no books on the subject in the church library. There were no models to follow. At Bible college there was no course called Bus Ministry 101 or Sunday School 101. I received no formal training for the kind of ministry I was doing, but deep within my soul I knew that children just like me needed to be reached. I also knew why they needed the Lord. The fact that I didn't have a step-by-step plan was irrelevant. I just had to get out there and make it happen.

When I was nineteen years old, I was told, "Bill, you have the largest bus ministry in our denomination."

"You've got to be kidding!" I responded. "I'm just learning how to get started."

To me, visiting a boy or girl in their home and bringing children to church was what Sunday school ministry was all about. Big numbers didn't matter. They were just a byproduct of doing what you were supposed to do.

Later, when I began to travel the nation, I realized that out of thousands of churches, only a handful were aggressively reaching the young people, or anyone for that matter, in their communities. In most cases a weekly routine was more important than renewal or revival. Maintaining the status quo was preferable to creativity and change.

Waiting for the "Call"

THE OLDER I become the more I realize that if people are going to be transformed, they are going to have to change the way they look at life itself.

At a recent missions convention the congregation was singing that old missions song, "I'll go where you want me to go, dear Lord." I thought for a moment about what we were singing, and it didn't make any sense. Most of the people in that auditorium weren't going anywhere. I knew it. They knew it, too. But they kept on singing words that were essentially meaningless. It's what they'd always done.

We need to get alone with the Lord and re-evaluate how our lives are being spent. I am not suggesting that people sell their possessions and move into a ghetto. What we do is not for everybody. But they should be willing to respond when they see a need where they are.

I live a life that is worlds apart from that of most Americans. That doesn't mean anybody is right or wrong; it just means we're different.

Only a short subway ride from Bushwick there are Wall Street executives who hold regular prayer meetings and Bible studies in the corporate boardrooms of Manhattan. Their work is as important as mine. They are ministering to people whom I will never meet.

In my travels I am often asked to be a guest on both Christian and secular television talk shows. Regardless of the program, the questions are usually the same. I can almost guarantee that within the first minute I will be asked, "How did God call you to New York?"

Once, on a live program in the Midwest, I responded to the question by saying, "God didn't call me to New York."

The host, with a rather puzzled look on his face, turned to the camera and said, "We'll be right back after this important message." And we went to a commercial.

Whose Child Is This?

Let me explain what I meant when I said that.

So many people depend on what we have come to know as the "call" of God or the "voice" of God. But when circumstances don't line up with what they feel is right, they fail to take any action at all.

If you are waiting for a supernatural revelation or a bolt from the blue to guide your future, you will likely wait forever. I have met scores of sincere people who have waited for a lifetime for God to speak to them. They think, *If I don't hear the voice of the Lord, I should not get involved in ministry.*

Countless well-meaning Christians have lived and died waiting for God to call them to something—and they never did anything while they were waiting. God can certainly speak through a burning bush or a pillar of fire, but we don't need to wait for such a sign. I wrote an article once titled "What Do You Do While You're Waiting for the Bush to Catch Fire?"

The great tragedy of missions in America is that many Christians believe missionaries are people who have seen visions and who have experienced supernatural encounters with God.

What would you do if your home caught on fire and your child was still inside? Would you say, "I'm not going in until the Lord tells me to"? No! You would rush in immediately because your child needed to be saved. That is the same motivation I felt in deciding to come to New York. I believe the need is the call. It's actually pretty simple. We've just made it complicated like so many other things in life.

"Why Not Me?"

WHEN I SAW the condition of the children in the ghettos of New York, it was not necessary for God to grab me by the shoulders and speak with a thunderous voice, "Bill Wilson, I want you to move to Bushwick."

I looked at the situation and knew immediately that somebody had to step forward. "Lord," I said, "it might as well be me. I think I can live there. I can work hard; I can trust You." If you've got to live anyway, live where you can help someone.

Let me repeat it again: The need was the call.

Most Christians, if you press them to discuss it, will admit to you exactly what their responsibility is as a Christian. When Christ gave the Great Commission, He said, "Go into all the world and preach the gospel to every creature. He who believes and is baptized will be saved; but he who does not believe will be condemned" (Mark 16:15–16).

The Lord did not say, "When I call you, I want you to go." He simply said, "Go!" Now we all know that, but for whatever reason it just hasn't clicked.

Today Christians have made soulwinning an option. Millions sit in their Sunday morning pews and say, "If people want to do that, fine. If they don't, that's fine, too." It's not fine. Instead of taking God at His Word, they check to see whether what they are doing feels comfortable.

Much of what I do is filled with stress and pain. I don't particularly enjoy living in Bushwick. I'm not sure anybody does. But we do it. It's not something that's been a lifelong goal for any of us. I've talked with thousands of people in the ghetto, and I rarely find someone who loves the neighborhood.

Why do I live and minister here? Because somebody has to do it. I did not respond to an audible "call." I responded to a desperate situation.

Do you want a call from God? You can have it immediately by opening your eyes to a specific need that surrounds you. Then step forward and throw your entire life into the project. That is how you respond to God's call.

The Choice Is Ours

I MAY BE ministering to larger numbers of young people today than I was in the 1970s, but the *need* is what motivated me then and is what continues to energize my life now. People at every level of society should look in the mirror and ask, *Am I satisfied with my life? Am I fulfilled each day by what I do?*

Each of us lives by the choices we make. Even those who reside in urban ghettos and complain about the conditions choose to remain with their families and friends. It is the only environment they really know.

Life is more than a tennis match, but one thing is certain: The ball is in our court. We can choose to live as we do or move to a higher level, saying, "I can do better. I can achieve more."

We can follow the path of least resistance, or we can take God at His Word and prepare for an eternity with Him.

I don't plan to reach the age of sixty-five and say, "I wish I had the chance to do it over again."

Instead, I am giving it 110 percent today. Today—not worrying about what I can do or what I will be doing next month or next year—but what I am doing today. Right now. The success of Metro Church is certainly not because I am clever, resourceful or intelligent. I just found a need that I believe in, and I have given my heart and soul to make a difference.

When you make a total commitment, there is a price to be paid. The cost may be higher than you ever imagined.

It's like some of you ladies who go window-shopping. You see this beautiful dress in the window; you go inside; you get to the dress rack; and what's the first thing you look at? The price tag, of course!

You look at it and casually go to another dress rack or another store. Now wait a minute. Don't miss this. What happened? Did the desire to have the dress change? No! You just don't want to pay the price, that's all.

That's the way it is in Christianity. We all want something to happen. We pray God will use us to help make it happen. The opportunity comes, and we choke. Why? Because it's going to cost us.

Is there always a price to pay? You better believe it! And for some of us the price has been higher than we want to admit. It's all relative. But don't embarrass yourself by going around saying you want to be used of God if you're not willing to go to the cash register with it. It happens all the time. You look pretty stupid carrying an opportunity back and putting it on the shelf.

Many times I have asked people, "Would you be willing to give your life for the cause of Christ?"

"Yes" is the usual reply, because that is the "right" answer. But they don't mean it. When the storm clouds build and the ship begins to toss, they are the first to abandon the boat. It is easy to talk about commitment, but rarely do we meet people who demonstrate it.

When Dave Rudenis saw me sitting on the culvert in Pinellas Park, Florida, he didn't have to pray about what he needed to do. He just saw a young boy whom nobody else wanted, and that was the call of God for him that day.

Dave didn't say, "Lord, should I pay for this boy to go to a Christian youth camp next week, or shouldn't I?" He knew instinctively what was needed in my life and made an instant decision to help. Fortunately, what was a normal response for him resulted in a life-changing transformation for me. It was at that youth camp on a Wednesday night that I met Jesus. And because of that experience and the events that followed, I am doing what I do today.

The Lord does not intend for you to sit idly by and wait for answers. He doesn't intend for you to ask, "Should I or shouldn't I?"

The Leper's Decision

DO YOU REMEMBER the dilemma that faced the four lepers who were sitting outside the city gate of Samaria in the Book of 2 Kings?

Most of you know that in Old Testament times one of the most common forms of warfare was to surround a city, thereby cutting off the enemy's water and food supplies. That's what the Syrians did in Samaria, and the people were facing starvation.

The four lepers were having a serious discussion regarding their plight.

> They said to one another, "Why are we sitting here until we die? If we say, 'We will enter the city,' the famine is in the city, and we shall die there. And if we sit here, we die also. Now therefore, come, let us surrender to the army of the Syrians. If they keep us alive, we shall live; and if they kill us, we shall only die."
>
> —2 KINGS 7:3–4

Whose Child Is This?

Have you ever been in a situation where everything you have lived for was suddenly coming to an end? Have you faced choices where every path seemed to lead to peril? What do you do when you don't know what to do? It is a tough place to be.

The four lepers came to the conclusion that to do something was better than waiting for death. They got up and started walking—straight toward the camp of the Syrian army.

Something amazing happened.

> And they rose at twilight to go to the camp of the Syrians; and when they had come to the outskirts of the Syrian camp, to their surprise no one was there. For the Lord had caused the army of the Syrians to hear the noise of chariots and the noise of horses—the noise of a great army; so they said to one another, "Look, the king of Israel has hired against us the kings of the Hittites and the kings of the Egyptians to attack us!" Therefore they arose and fled at twilight, and left the camp intact—their tents, their horses, and their donkeys—and they fled for their lives.
>
> —2 KINGS 7:5–7

When the lepers arrived at the camp, they went into one tent after another. There was food, drink and even gold, silver and clothing. They ran back to the city and shared the good news, and the people shouted for joy. The famine was over.

If you ever reach the point where you don't know what to do, the best risk is to go forward. That's what the apostle Paul did. He said, "Brethren, I do not count myself to have apprehended; but one thing I do, forgetting those things which are behind and reaching forward to those things which are ahead, I press toward the goal for the prize of the upward call of God in Christ Jesus" (Phil. 3:13–14).

Don't just talk about doing something; we've seen enough talkers in Christianity. Stand to your feet and begin to take action. You may not be able to change the world, but your actions can touch someone's life. The candle you hold may not provide light for the world, but it will brighten the life of a person in need. As

Eleanor Roosevelt said, "Better to light a candle than curse the darkness."

A Shining Light

ONE OF OUR Sunday schools is in Harlem, perhaps New York's most noted ghetto. On 126th Street there was a little boy who, day after day, took a little piece of a broken mirror and reflected beams of light up to an apartment in a tenement house.

"What do you think you are doing?" asked a policeman who had been watching the boy for several days. "Are you bothering those people up there?"

"No, sir," said the little boy. "That apartment is where I live."

"Then why are you shining that light up there?" the policeman wanted to know.

"Well, mister, that is where my little brother is. He is six years old and has never been able to walk. My mother doesn't have enough money to buy him a wheelchair."

He continued, "If we bring him outside and carry him, the kids throw rocks at him. He doesn't want to come down. So every day I stand here and try to shine some light into his room, because that is the only light he ever sees."

In a land that has been abundantly blessed, there are people everywhere who are waiting for a sign that somebody cares.

Let their need become God's call to you.

Bill always takes time to share valuable wisdom with the next generation.

CHAPTER NINE

"Do I Really Care?"

I WAS HAVING A quick lunch at McDonald's on Saturday between my bus routes. Ruby and her brother and sisters were there, passing the time before their bus came by to take them to Sunday school. She used to ride my bus, but their building had been taken over by drug dealers. They had to move, so she rode someone else's bus. But our friendship remained strong.

As we were talking I noticed that the frame was broken on her glasses and one of the lenses kept falling out. It happened several times, but she would put it back in and keep on laughing and talking.

Ruby started coming to Metro Church when her family lived in Brooklyn. Every week she and her brother and sisters would ride the subways from South Bronx to be in Sunday school—changing trains three times in the process.

When I walked back to my bus, ready to pick up another load for the next church service, Ruby ran over and handed me her glasses. "Pastor Bill, could you fix these?" she asked.

"Let me take a look," I answered.

There wasn't much time, but I rushed into a store and bought a roll of silver duct tape—not an ideal glasses-fixing tool, but it was all that was available. It will mend almost anything. I taped the lens to her frame the best I could, and she was on her way.

Whose Child Is This?

A few seconds later she was back. Ruby hopped up the stairs of my bus and said, "I want to thank you for fixing my glasses. My mom said she didn't have time to fix them. I love you." Then she gave me a big hug and was gone.

I recently performed Ruby's wedding. She married a fine young man in the church. It's great to see these kids grow up. But it all came from someone just caring. Most folks just don't want to take the time to fix glasses. I guess everyone's just busy. Too bad, isn't it?

The Greatest Lesson

I GREW UP like Ruby. By their actions, people in my life were always saying, "I don't have time for you."

"I don't have time to get you a new pair of shoes"—so I wore shoes with holes in them, and everybody laughed.

"I don't have time to take you to the clothing store"—so I would sit with my hands on my knees to cover the holes in my blue jeans.

It doesn't take much effort to pause for a moment and say, "Sure, I'll fix your glasses for you."

In a busy week of building props, preparing messages, visiting families, driving bus routes and flying to speaking engagements, it would be easy to say to a child, "I don't have time."

Long ago I realized that though I may have a successful ministry and a first-rate presentation of the gospel, taking the time to put my arm around a child and actually listen, not just act like I'm listening, is more effective than any lesson I will ever present.

When my life was transformed as a teenager, I began to attend Sunday school week after week. I must have heard two or three hundred lessons—but I still cannot specifically recall one of them. And I've really tried.

What I do remember is the time our teacher invited us to breakfast on a Saturday morning and treated me as a special person. He picked us up. He talked to us. He cared. I can also vividly recall sitting around a Royal Ranger campfire cooking marshmallows and talking with the leader one-on-one.

"Do I Really Care?"

I wish there was a quick fix or an easy answer for reaching young people who are hurting. There is not. But every day we meet another Ruby or another Bill who needs our time and attention. That is where we must begin.

Teaching With Fire

DO I *REALLY* care? That is the question we must all ask ourselves. I can tell you almost everything you need to know about Sunday school teaching. I have done it for years. But classroom techniques and instructional strategies are a waste of time unless you deeply care for the young people you are attempting to reach.

It starts on the inside. Without a fire that burns in your bones, it doesn't matter how many teacher's quarterlies you have read or how many years you have been in the classroom.

Henrietta Mears, an author who spent a lifetime in Christian education, has said, "The teacher has not taught until the pupil has learned."

How do they learn? When children love the messenger, they are open to the message. That is why caring must always precede communication. If people don't like you, they're not going to listen to you. It's that simple.

The answer to a successful Sunday school program cannot be found in the careful lesson plans that have been written and published for decades. Some people treat their teacher's manual as if it were inspired and ordained by God—but most of the time it has never been tested on kids!

Every week the lesson plan at Metro Sunday school becomes written curriculum that is used around the world. It is not published before it is presented but only after it has been designed, developed and demonstrated.

What we have developed may be the most exciting, effective material you can find, but it will be as boring as 4 A.M. if it is not presented by people who have a fire burning within their spirits.

If you don't "feel" the lesson, your classroom will become as dead as a funeral parlor. It is only when your "thus saith the Lord" is accompanied by a heart of compassion and caring that the message

117

comes through. People of every age will respond by feeling what we feel. When we don't care, they won't either.

Every week when I deliver what we work so hard to prepare, I treat that hour as if it were heaven or hell—because that is exactly what it is.

Speaking to a group of Christian educators recently, I was rather blunt. "If you look at your class as anything less than life or death, you do not deserve to be a teacher. If you walk into the classroom ten minutes late, week after week, you need to resign. You wouldn't come in late on your job all the time, but I'd venture to guess that some of you do it on Sunday." There is no excuse. I'm sorry, there just isn't.

What does this have to do with Christian education? Everything. Sunday school teachers need to come face to face with the depth of their love and concern. If people don't know how much you care, they couldn't care less about how much you know.

You can be a teacher for thirty years and have a dozen achievement certificates on your walls, but they are meaningless if you don't have a heart for your class. Do you cry when they cry? Are you touched by their feelings? The Bible says Jesus was not only touched by people's infirmities, but by the very feelings of the infirmities.

The world has grown tired of the games being played in many churches. What they are searching for is something they recognize instantly. It is called reality.

As Christians we have learned the right words to the right songs and have become experts on the topic of love and forgiveness. We have practiced how to smile and how to show concern. We can even yawn and praise the Lord at the same time. Isn't that amazing? There is just one problem. People recognize a phony when they see one, and shallowness is exposed faster than most people imagine.

The days of attempting to "fake it 'til we make it" need to end. Either we are in this thing for the right reasons—and for the long haul—or we need to get out of the way and let someone else take over.

The world is watching. They've seen enough scandals. Now they want to see if what we believe really works. A hurting child is only looking for one thing—someone with compassion and concern. They are looking for love that is shared heart to heart.

Are we teaching because lives need to be transformed? Or are we there only because no one else would take the class? It's hard to believe that some teachers can present a lesson week after week and never take the time to talk personally with one student. In most cases they've never been in the kids' homes or don't even know the kids.

What conclusion can I draw about a Sunday school teacher who never visits a home, never phones an absentee and never invites someone to attend the class? Do they really care?

Life is too short and the problems are too great to hurriedly spend fifteen or twenty minutes every Saturday night putting some slop-job lesson together. It is time we stop thinking about teaching the lesson and begin to consider how we can reach out with love and concern for a child.

We're not supposed to be teaching lessons; we're teaching people.

God's Special People

FOLLOWING A SUNDAY morning service in Los Angeles, a lady asked if she could speak with me for a moment. That morning I spoke on the importance of perseverance and what it means to "hang in there."

"I listened to your message about never giving up, but I don't know if it's possible for me," the woman said. "I have leukemia. And I also have four little children. When I die, what is going to happen to my kids?"

I sat down on a pew in the front of that church and cried with her. That was all I could do. I prayed, "Lord, place Your arms around this family and show them Your love."

Later, as I was flying home, I couldn't stop thinking about those kids who might soon be without a mother. *Who will look after them?* I wondered. *Will anybody really care?*

The Lord gives special attention to people in need, and I feel He expects us to do the same.

For years I was taught to believe that God is not partial and that He cares equally for everyone. I suppose it is an extension of the verse that says, "For there is no partiality with God" (Rom. 2:11). But while the Lord loves us all, Scripture makes it clear that the Lord knows our unique and special needs and even calls us by name.

Immediately following the crucifixion of Jesus, He was buried in a rock-hewn tomb. On the third day Mary Magdalene and some others went to the sepulcher to anoint the body with some sweet spices they had purchased.

> Very early in the morning, on the first day of the week, they came to the tomb when the sun had risen. And they said among themselves, "Who will roll away the stone from the door of the tomb for us?" But when they looked up, they saw that the stone had been rolled away—for it was very large. And entering the tomb, they saw a young man clothed in a long white robe sitting on the right side; and they were alarmed. But he said to them, "Do not be alarmed. You seek Jesus of Nazareth, who was crucified. He is risen! He is not here. See the place where they laid Him."
>
> —MARK 16:2–6

Then the angel spoke these words: "But go, tell His disciples— *and Peter*—that He is going before you into Galilee; there you will see Him, as He said to you" (v. 7, emphasis added).

Peter was one of the disciples, yet God singled him out. The women who heard the words of the angel were to tell the good news of the resurrection of Christ to the disciples—but specifically they were to tell Peter.

Why did God call him by name? Why was Peter so special? It was as if the angel were saying, "If you tell anybody, be sure to tell him."

A Broken Promise

THE CHARACTER OF Peter can only be described as brash, energetic and impulsive. He was so reckless in his behavior that he once cut off a man's ear (John 18:26).

His "humanity" made him one of the most beloved members of the apostolic band. But there was another side to Peter. He could be swayed easily. Some viewed him as being fickle—even cowardly and obnoxious.

Peter made great promises to the Lord but didn't keep his word. The disciple said, "Lord, I am ready to go with You, both to prison and to death" (Luke 22:33).

Jesus looked at him and said, "I tell you, Peter, the rooster shall not crow this day before you will deny three times that you know Me" (v. 34).

When they arrested the Lord, Peter followed at a distance. The soldiers made a fire in the courtyard of the place they had taken Jesus. Peter edged closer. "And a certain servant girl, seeing him as he sat by the fire, looked intently at him and said, 'This man was also with Him.' But he denied Him, saying, 'Woman, I do not know Him'" (vv. 56–57).

And after a little while another saw him and said, "'You also are of them.' But Peter said, 'Man, I am not!' Then after about an hour had passed, another confidently affirmed, saying, 'Surely this fellow also was with Him, for he is a Galilean.' But Peter said, 'Man, I do not know what you are saying!' Immediately, while he was still speaking, the rooster crowed" (vv. 58–60).

It was then that Jesus turned and looked directly at Peter. The disciple fled from the courtyard, crying bitterly.

Peter must have endured great pain at the death and burial of Jesus. In his heart he truly loved the Lord and was no doubt feeling great remorse for denying Christ. He knew he had blown it—badly. Nobody needed to tell him; he knew it.

Peter—actually despised because of his lack of loyalty to the Lord—was in the same room with the other disciples when Mary told them the good news. He was the one who then ran to the tomb. This is stated clearly in Luke.

But God especially wanted Peter to know that Christ was alive. He was saying, "Tell him—he needs to know that today."

And he needed to know that more at that point in his life than he ever had before.

Not only did Peter receive the news, but he began a spiritual journey with Christ that completely restored him. Peter became a man of stability, humility and courageous service for God.

Whose Child Is This?

There are times in life when, like Peter, we need the Lord's special attention. I certainly have had those times, and He has never failed me. I believe the Lord was listening when the lady in Los Angeles asked, "What is going to happen to my kids?"

"You're Not Allowed"

NOT FAR FROM our church on Jefferson and Troutman streets is one of the most dangerous areas in Brooklyn. The drug traffic is high, and prostitution is rampant. I've learned to survive in rough neighborhoods. But this area is beyond what even we consider marginal.

One night I was in the area with one of our staff members. Several "women of the street" recognized that we were from Metro Church. We began to talk with them about the Lord, and one of the women said, "We've done too much. God can't forgive us."

Her friend said, "Why should we ever go to church? There is no hope for us."

You could see in their eyes that they actually believed they had gone too far to be forgiven. Even sadder, there are Christians who feel the same way about other people.

On a Sunday evening in Oklahoma I arrived early at a church where I was to preach. I was standing in the back of the auditorium, listening to the choir as they rehearsed. Behind me the door of the church opened and a rather disheveled man walked in. I thought, *If he isn't a homeless bum, nobody is.* He looked like some of the guys we deal with in New York.

The man took off his little backpack, placed it on the pew and sat down.

Immediately an usher came into the auditorium and began to talk with the visitor. The man picked up his belongings and walked out.

I was curious to find out what happened, so I walked over to the usher and asked, "What did you say to that man?"

"I told him that we don't allow people like him in this church!"

When I was younger there was a little game I used to play. For my speaking engagements it seemed as if I would always arrive at the church just after the service had begun. I never meant to; it just happened. I would put down my suitcase in the lobby and walk around for a minute or two, still dressed in my traveling clothes—jeans, T-shirt and tennis shoes.

Here's what I learned. When I was dressed in old clothes, looking like a nobody, it was rare that someone would shake my hand or welcome me to the church. Then I would find a place to put on a suit and tie, and people would begin to recognize me as the guest speaker. "God bless you," they would say. "It's good to have you here tonight."

The only thing that made a difference was the fact that I had put on a suit. That somehow made me palatable for them. In my jeans and T-shirt, I talked the same, I walked the same and I acted the same. But because I did not look like somebody they wanted to be with, I was not welcome.

What Does God See?

HAVE YOU EVER wondered what it would be like to be hated because of the color of your skin? I can tell you from experience because I am one of the few white people who live in my neighborhood. When I first moved to Bushwick, it wasn't fun. I've been spit upon, hassled and called pretty much everything.

Prejudice comes in many forms. After years in the ghetto I have become sensitive to it and understand the tension it causes. I can identify with a little child who is "different"—who is cursed and taunted because of a cultural gap. It's not fun being a kid and not being able to understand or explain why people dislike you.

Each week I am in a different part of the country and see how people everywhere stick close to their cookie-cutter group. They only feel comfortable with people just like themselves and are quick to judge those who don't meet their standards.

If we attempted to have a church in Brooklyn for people who were "good enough," our doors would never open. But I thank God that our altars are stained with the tears of those who obviously need Him the most.

Last year dozens in our adult congregation died of AIDS. We watch them slowly perish because of "the virus." Before we conducted his funeral, one of the HIV-positive men told me, "Pastor Bill, I went to fifteen other churches in Brooklyn. When they found out I had AIDS, they all asked me not to come back." Then he said, "You people are the only ones who took me in."

Maybe I'm missing something, but I thought that is what a church is supposed to do.

Hungry and Crying

WHEN WE MAKE our weekly visits in large apartment buildings, we usually begin by taking an elevator to the top floor, and then we work our way down. One building is fifteen stories high, and when I reached the twelfth floor, I heard a child crying.

It was the floor where one of our workers lives, and a small boy—one who rode my bus each week—was sitting in front of his apartment door, waiting for his mother to return.

It was about 4:30 in the afternoon, and school had been out for a little while.

"Why are you crying?" I asked. Nobody was around, and it wasn't a good situation.

"My mom is not home, and she didn't make me a lunch today. I haven't had anything to eat, and I'm hungry. I don't know what to do."

I took him with me to a corner pizza shop and bought him a slice and a soda. He stayed with me for the rest of my visits that day, and we went back to the church. The boy followed me like a shadow.

Every few minutes we would dial the number of his house to see if his mother had returned. It was about eleven o'clock that night when we finally reached her. There was no "thank you" from the mother or the slightest expression of concern for the boy when we took him home. Instead she cursed at him and slapped him across the face for drawing attention to her stupidity.

What do you do when a child is crying? You realize that someone has to care.

A man in South Bronx once tried to explain to me why his beautiful neighborhood had deteriorated into a scene of urban blight. "Nobody cares anymore," he said. "This used to be a wonderful place. Then apathy set in, and we never recovered."

Apathy is a contagious disease that spreads quickly and can kill everything in its path—not just buildings, but families. It's not confined to the ghetto. You can find it in our suburbs, in our schools and in our churches.

When people care more for themselves than for people around them, society begins to crumble.

A minister I knew very well recently passed away. What I will always remember about him was a question he had printed on his church stationery. Under a picture of a little boy and girl holding hands was the caption, "What does it cost to save a child?"

The longer I live the more I realize that the cost of reaching a child cannot be measured in dollars and cents. We can only rescue a boy or a girl by giving them a portion of our life.

In a nation that has been so abundantly blessed, we wonder why so many are desperate for help. It is difficult to comprehend how a land with more than four hundred thousand churches could fall into such moral decay.

Whatever happened to the Reformation that began when Martin Luther tacked his ninety-five theses to the door of the Wittenburg church? What happened to the revival that came through the circuit-riding preaching of John and Charles Wesley? Why are there so few soulwinning churches in the denominations those movements spawned?

When Christians stop caring, the church begins to die. Organizations don't care; people do. A congregation whose main concern is its own comfort and traditions will soon lose its reason for being. That is why today's evangelical churches need to keep a passion for souls. It is the only hope for the church.

Church bulletins and marquees declare, "We love you." But the attitude that is conveyed once the unlovely actually step inside is, "We love you, but just don't sit next to me."

When the collection is taken for missions, many respond only out of guilt. It is much easier to put a dollar in the plate than to actually get physically involved in ministry.

Before he died, Mahatma Gandhi, the noted leader in India,

said, "The only thing that ever kept me from being a Christian was Christians." Sad, isn't it? Sad, because it's true.

It is time to stop looking in the mirror at our facade and our personality. Instead we need to ask God to shine His searchlight directly into our heart. We need to examine our motives for ministry. Are we looking for applause, or do we genuinely care about the souls around us?

The Lord is not asking that we personally rescue the entire world. He is more concerned that we begin by caring for someone who needs our love. We didn't come to the ghetto to be ministered to, but to minister.

Will It Make a Difference?

IN AUSTRALIA THERE is a beach where at certain times each year thousands of starfish are washed up on the sand. Usually at night, at high tide, a large wave will bring them in so far that the water won't carry them back out. Then, as the sun shines on the starfish, they slowly dry out and die.

One morning a tourist came out of his hotel for a jog at dawn. Down on the beach he noticed a little boy picking up stranded starfish and throwing them back into the sea. But there were thousands of them up and down the shore.

The man ran up to the boy and said, "I know what you're doing, and I think I know why you're doing it. But there are thousands of starfish here and miles of beach. Do you really think that what you are doing is going to make a difference?"

The boy said, "I don't know. But I think it will make a difference to this one."

And he picked up another starfish and threw it into the sea.

The Lord is searching the land for people like this little boy, who care enough to minister to one at a time. Those are the ones who are special in His sight.

Consider the words of Jesus about His return. "When the Son of Man comes in His glory, and all the holy angels with Him, then He will sit on the throne of His glory. All the nations will be gathered before Him, and He will separate them one from another, as a shepherd divides his sheep from the goats. And He will set the sheep on His right hand, but the goats on the left" (Matt. 25:31–33).

On what basis will they be separated? "Then the King will say to those on His right hand, 'Come, you blessed of My Father, inherit the kingdom prepared for you from the foundation of the world: for I was hungry and you gave Me food; I was thirsty and you gave Me drink; I was a stranger and you took Me in; I was naked and you clothed Me; I was sick and you visited Me; I was in prison and you came to Me'" (vv. 34–36).

Scripture tells us that the righteous will answer Him, saying, "Lord, when did we see You hungry and feed You, or thirsty and give You drink? When did we see You a stranger and take You in, or naked and clothe You? Or when did we see You sick, or in prison, and come to You?" (vv. 37–39).

The Lord will answer and say to them, "'Assuredly, I say to you, inasmuch as you did it to one of the least of these My brethren, you did it to Me.' Then He will also say to those on the left hand, 'Depart from Me, you cursed, into the everlasting fire prepared for the devil and his angels: for I was hungry and you gave Me no food; I was thirsty and you gave Me no drink; I was a stranger and you did not take Me in, naked and you did not clothe Me, sick and in prison and you did not visit Me'" (vv. 40–43).

"Then they also will answer Him, saying, 'Lord, when did we see You hungry or thirsty or a stranger or naked or sick or in prison, and did not minister to You?' Then He will answer them, saying, 'Assuredly, I say to you, inasmuch as you did not do it to one of the least of these, you did not do it to Me.' And these will go away into everlasting punishment, but the righteous into eternal life" (vv. 44–46).

"I've Got Eighty-four Cents"

THERE IS A little boy who attends our Sunday school who lives near the church. His mother is a drug addict we often see standing in front of the grocery store across the street from our church.

127

Whose Child Is This?

Starting several weeks before his tenth birthday, he began to ask members of our staff, "Do you think you could have a party for me when I am ten?"

This boy had never had a birthday party in his life, and it was all he could think about. One afternoon he came into our office and talked to one of our bus captains. "Here, look at this," the boy said as he poured a pile of pennies on the table. "I've got eighty-four cents. Will that be enough to have a party here in the office?"

He told the staff member that he had been collecting the pennies on the streets for several weeks.

We bought a few little cupcakes and made some juice and some sandwiches for the celebration. We even hung some streamers on the wall and sang "Happy Birthday."

During that time several of our staff members were going through a rough time in their own lives. It would have been much easier for them to say, "We can't do that. We don't have the time. It's stupid. If we can't do it right, let's not do anything at all."

At the party I noticed tears in the eyes of our staff when they realized how much this meant to this little boy.

Later that day I asked the bus captain, "What made you decide to have the party?"

He said, "Somebody had to do something."

Somebody did.

Somebody cared.

Metro's staff takes the gospel to the streets with cube vans specially modified to include a stage, sound system and everything else needed to deliver the message.

CHAPTER TEN

The Most Exciting Hour of the Week

WHY IS SUNDAY school attendance dropping?" I asked a pastor in Illinois. He was not the first Christian leader I had asked. For the past few years I have posed the question to hundreds of Christian educators and church leaders. I wanted to know the reason for the dramatic decline in those attending Sunday school. Here is what I have found.

The number one reason given for decreasing enrollment was the perception that our people are not really concerned with outreach anymore.

This is true for mainline, evangelical and even many charismatic churches. A growing Sunday school takes a commitment of time and energy to reach beyond the existing members of the congregation. Many churches have been involved in an internal battle between serving a close-knit group of families and aggressively reaching out to new people. Unfortunately, the "we're happy as we are, us four and no more" crowd has won many of those skirmishes, and soulwinning pastors have moved on.

The second reason given for dwindling numbers is that the classes are not relevant.

We can no longer expect to capture the attention of young people with a boring one-hour lecture on a topic that is unrelated to their life. It is not going to happen.

Whose Child Is This?

Today's children live in a video generation where everything is moving fast—from *Sesame Street* to *Robo-Cops*. Music videos are edited with one-, two- and three-second cuts. Boom. Boom. Boom.

I am not saying we have to be in direct competition with productions that cost millions of dollars to generate. But I believe we have to become relevant in both our content and our presentation. That means becoming creative. Most teachers would be amazed at what would happen if they assigned next week's lesson to five students who were to prepare a three-minute presentation on their assigned topic. Not only would those involved learn the material, but they would have the undivided attention of the class.

Today's young people are dealing with questions and issues that we never dreamed would be discussed. Questions such as, "When does a baby become a baby? At conception? At two months? At birth?" First-graders in New York are being taught about homosexual and lesbian lifestyles and how they're just "another kind of love."

At younger and younger ages our beliefs are being challenged—in the school, in the media and in conversations with peers. Young people want to know what the church says about divorce, AIDS and dozens of other contemporary issues.

Children today are worrying about topics we could only have imagined a few years ago. Here is an example.

In Brooklyn, some older teens on Knickerbocker Avenue were taking powdered cocaine and wiping it on the back of the stickers children lick and paste in storybooks.

The youngsters who bought the little books were suddenly being rushed to emergency rooms in Wyckoff and Woodhull—hospitals in our neighborhood. The children were overdosing and having a variety of medical problems. Fortunately, they traced the source of the problem to the teens and arrested them.

As a child I didn't have to deal with those kinds of concerns. But at Metro we face such reality every day.

In our neighborhood, girls who are eleven and twelve years old are sexually active and having children. It's kids having kids. The parents can't cope with their own daughters—much less a new baby in the home. There is no guidance and no direction.

We try to convince ourselves that we're relevant, but we are not.

In most churches we are still answering questions that nobody is even asking. Our inner-city curriculum has been criticized because the stories are sometimes violent and may not have a happy ending. Life doesn't always have a happy ending. That's just reality.

Here is another frequent response to my question of why Sunday school attendance is dropping: "There is no long-range planning," a teacher in Cleveland told me. "We still have Sunday school, but we don't have either an educational or a spiritual goal."

Many people are like the proverbial fanatic who said, "I've lost my way, but I've doubled my speed." We want to make a success of our efforts, but we don't know where we want to go, let alone how to get there.

The fact that Sunday school attendance is decreasing should never be an excuse to lessen our resolve to bring the message of Christ to young people. We can list all of the reasons or excuses possible, but the truth remains that children desperately need moral, ethical and spiritual training as a foundation for life.

Can Church Be Fun?

I HAVE BEEN asked repeatedly, "If Sunday school attendance is declining, why has Metro Church bucked that trend? Why are you growing so rapidly?"

There are many reasons, but one is clear. We believe that Sunday school should be and can be the most exciting hour of the week.

It makes no difference when you meet or where. You don't have to schedule classes on Sunday, or even hold your meetings in a church. Of far greater importance is the preparation you give to making every session the best it can be.

We have reached thousands of children who did not know about Jesus and had never heard the words "Sunday school" before. We had to begin with the basics and build from there.

I've been asked, "Bill, if you hold your session on Saturday, why don't you call it Saturday school?"

I believe that Sunday school is a generic term that denotes something spiritual and is related to the church. Our Sidewalk Sunday School programs operate in the middle of the week, and those who attend don't worry about what day it's held; they only know it is an exciting place to be and they want to come.

There is a valid reason that children in our neighborhood count the hours until our bus arrives each week. They know that what they are going to hear and see in the next hour and thirty minutes will be the highlight of their week.

I make no apology for my belief that Sunday school should be fun. Why should young people grow up with the notion that church is boring? They can only come to that conclusion when it is dull and lifeless.

We present the gospel in a stimulating, often "electric" atmosphere. It's fun, but it is still church. When it comes time for the message, the students are quiet and receptive. We also know the limits of their attention span. That is why we choose our words carefully and focus our weekly objective for maximum impact. We take one primary topic that week and illustrate it five or six different ways. We're saying the same thing—just showing it in varied ways.

You may say, "Our church is small. It would be impossible to duplicate a program like yours."

I am not suggesting that you need a twenty-foot video projection screen and a live band to capture the attention of children. Everything is relative. To make Sunday school the most exciting hour in your community depends on what is currently being presented. The introduction of just one life-size costumed character next week may provide the spark that gives you momentum. My files are filled with letters from Sunday school teachers in small churches who tell me how their program has been revitalized.

"Don't Play Around"

AT METRO SUNDAY school we build each week's lesson around a simple theme or principle. We do our best to take one point and drive it home. Our objective is to make the application so clear that they will apply it to their lives and never forget it. Let me give some examples.

A few weeks ago our theme for the day was, "Don't get close to sin."

The Most Exciting Hour of the Week

On our video projector we showed a short clip from a film of sea lions playing on some rocks near a whale. Suddenly the whale turned and swallowed one of the fun-loving sea lions. Even after that happened, the other sea lions continued to swim around the whale.

During the film clip we said, "Kids, if you play around with sin, it will turn on you."

Then we projected a "Pac-Man" game on the screen with a little monster gobbling up anything that came too close. The children got the point.

In my message I talked about things these street-smart kids know very well. I said, "Let me tell you about two boys who were playing on the roof of a tenement building. They began jumping from one building to the next. It was fun while it lasted, but then one boy didn't quite make it. He fell to his death."

I gave a similar example of two boys who were jumping between the cars of a subway train until one tragically tripped and fell.

Next I talked about what happens to young people who think it is cool to make deliveries or sell for drug dealers.

In my closing prayer I asked the children to repeat after me: "I don't want to play around with sin. I don't want to end up like the people on my block. Help me to remember what I've heard today. I want to stay close to You, Jesus. I know You died for me. I want to live for You. Amen."

Can They See It?

WE ALWAYS USE visual objects to illustrate the point. Eighty-three percent of everything we learn comes through our eyes. Children have to see what you're saying. I may hold up two glasses filled with clear liquid and say, "They look exactly alike, but one contains water and the other is filled with vinegar. That is how Satan plays tricks on you."

In a theme that involved Noah and the ark, we got their attention with a Teenage Mutant Ninja Turtle illustration.

We have produced hundreds of short skits—like "G.I Joel," based on the Old Testament prophet.

Every week I want the boys and girls to visualize the theme and

135

commit it to memory. The lesson is not based on three or four points—just one.

Along with the weekly objectives, we have general themes we use for several weeks. One series of lessons was "Life Under Construction." The stage looked like a half-finished building, and the staff wore plastic hard hats. One week an important point was illustrated by rearranging words written on giant cardboard building blocks.

We often give prizes to those who can be the first to repeat last week's theme word for word.

"What was the lesson last week?" I'll ask.

A little boy or girl will run up to a microphone and say, "What you feed grows, and what you starve dies."

"That's it! Perfect!" And we will give the child a small gift. It's positive motivation.

Every week there is something new. There are contests, races and quizzes about Bible stories and memory verses.

On special days like Easter or Thanksgiving we tie the message to the celebration. Last year, on Mother's Day, we printed a special card from Metro Church for each child to take home.

My message that day was centered on the theme that we should love our mother regardless of her actions. I told the children, "Love what is good, disregard what is bad and do your best to lead your mother to Jesus."

After the lesson a worker noticed a little girl who was crying. The child was crying because her mother had just been shot and killed—and the mother did not know the Lord.

Our staff gave the child special love that day.

Regardless of the theme, the outline for the message is often the same:

1. This is who Jesus is.
2. This is who the devil is.
3. This is why this city is like it is and why people on your block are doing what they are doing.
4. If you want to be like that, fine. If you don't, here is what you can do: Accept Jesus as your Savior and let

Him make something of your life.

We do it again and again, week after week.

In our presentation of the gospel we place our emphasis on the love of God. The people in our neighborhoods don't need us to tell them they are living in sin. They are smart enough to know it. What they need is for somebody to tell them, "No matter what you have done, the Lord loves you and is ready to forgive you."

Not every lesson is totally spiritual. Many of these children have never learned the basic values of life. We have presented special sessions that teach the concept of a work ethic, how to read and write, how to hold a conversation and how to be socially acceptable—including how to take a bath.

It is also important for young people to know that the values of both the church and the nation are founded on God's Word. The Ten Commandments and the Golden Rule are not words from history books, but they are to be practiced every day.

The lessons of life should be taught early. I love Robert Fulghum's book *All I Really Need to Know I Learned in Kindergarten*. That's where we learned to "share everything. Play fair. Don't hit people. Put things back where you found them"— and so much more.

A concept we try to instill in the children is: You don't want to be like everyone you see. You don't have to be a loser. You can accomplish anything you set your heart on. We tell them that Jesus is the One who makes it possible. "The Lord will be with you when no one else is there."

Today's Idols

LIVING MESSAGES CAN have a great impact.

I remember the day we did a presentation on one of the Ten Commandments—the dangers of worshiping idols. We wanted to drive home the point that idols were not just something the Israelites dealt with centuries ago but something we have to face today.

We constructed a large cross in the center of the stage. Kneeling before the cross was a group of teenagers, praying. I said to the audience, "Sometimes there are things in our life that are idols—things we put in front of God."

One by one the young people stood to their feet and walked behind a large screen to bring out something they were giving more importance to than the Lord.

The first teen brought out a television set, placed it before the cross and then fell to her knees. I said, "She put television in front of God. She attended church, but if there was something she wanted to see, she would not be found in the house of God."

Next was a young man who brought a poster of the Teenage Mutant Ninja Turtles. That was his idol. He hung it on the cross.

Then a teen hung some fancy clothes on the cross.

When the young people saw a cross covered up with the things that were important in their lives, the impact was strong. They realized that what they were worshiping was not pleasing to the Lord. The cross was not first place in their lives.

There was one particular moment when it seemed the message penetrated every heart in the room. It was as if a light bulb had been turned on inside them. *That's me!* they realized. *That's what I'm doing.*

Suddenly a spirit of anointing filled the room. You could feel the presence of God and the power of conviction. The Lord spoke directly to hundreds of young people, and lives were permanently transformed. This is Sunday school we're talking about now, not some revival.

On dozens of occasions visitors have stood in the back of our auditorium to observe Sunday school at Metro. We would like to be able to offer them a chair, but those are reserved for our most important guests—the children who ride our buses.

The observers have come from all over the world. The question they ask most often is, "How do you do this all the time?" They can see the energy it takes for just one Sunday school hour.

This ministry is a very physical one—tough, dirty, sweaty, hands-on work. It's very draining, both mentally and physically. The staff does not sit around all week sharpening pencils and shuffling papers. There are buses to be cleaned, props to be built and tenement buildings to be visited.

Where do the daily motivation and energy come from? The longer we are involved, the more we realize how much the children depend on us for their future. When you see the results of your ministry day after day, it makes you want to double and triple the effort. But even if we didn't see the results, the real issue is commitment. You don't entertain quitting. You can't. If you leave yourself an out in life when things get tough, you'll take it. It's human nature.

In the seminars I conduct around the country, people ask, "If you were to give me some advice about getting involved in ministry like this that makes a difference, what would it be?"

Here are ten basic principles of character development for ministry that I have learned, mostly the hard way, over the years.

Principle #1: *Build on your strengths.*

When I was young, people told me, "Bill, you need to improve on your weaknesses."

I tried their suggestion, but it didn't seem to work. I became slightly more proficient in a few areas, but there was no great leap forward in my life. I spent all my time preoccupied with all the things that weren't right in my life.

Then one day I found my strength—the ability to communicate with young people. When I concentrated on what I did best, great things began to unfold.

I'm not a five-talent man. I'm not even a three-talent man. I know that. But I've got a couple of things that I do very well. I told a group of Christian educators recently, "As far as being a Sunday school teacher is concerned, I'm probably one of the best."

That may sound a little brash, but the reason I say it is because I have diligently sought to be the best. Second place is not good enough. Does this mean we should ignore our faults and shortcomings? Absolutely not. But there has got to be a balance.

Take an inventory of the talents God has given you and make those abilities your launching pad. Then find your greatest strength and become a world-class champion. Yes, you can improve on areas that are weak, but you won't become a winner by being preoccupied with your faults.

139

You can rely on your strengths so much that you can literally talk yourself out of improvement in areas that need to be improved. On the other hand, you can let your weaknesses drain you of motivation.

I am amused at young ministers who attend a "pastor's school" and return to their communities trying to imitate their mentors. It won't work. Other people have special talents you will never possess. But you have unique abilities, too.

I still believe that the world's greatest Sunday school is yet to be built. I feel that the greatest class is yet to be taught. Someone, somewhere, will rise to the challenge.

Principle #2: *Do not get involved with fools.*

Proverbs 14:7; 1:5 and 9:8, along with every chapter in the Book of Hard Knocks, should give us insight into the kind of work that we are all involved in. And the kind of people we should avoid as much as possible.

There is great danger in being around a fool. If you are going to accomplish anything for the kingdom of God, you cannot afford to spend a whole lot of time with those kinds of people. Proverbs 13:20 clearly illustrates that the company you keep says a lot about you as a person, and it will be easily read by everyone around you.

Principle #3: *To be is more important than to do.*

In the early days of Yale University, when it was known as a Christian college, president Timothy Dwight decided that the school needed a department of chemistry. Most of the great chemists were still in Europe.

He looked over the records of Yale's students and found a young man named Benjamin Sulliman. He was a scholar with an outstanding record. More important, he was a man of great character and integrity.

The president said, "Ben, we would like to give you a scholarship to go to Europe, learn chemistry and return to Yale to teach."

Sulliman said, "But I don't know anything about chemistry."

Dwight said, "That does not matter. You can learn whatever you need to know. That's basic academics. You're the kind of person we want teaching in our school."

What you are is of far greater importance than what you can do.

The day I was to go for my ministerial ordination, I suddenly realized I had a problem. The night before, my only pair of shoes had been stolen from my van in Brooklyn.

So I arrived at the office of the district superintendent in a suit and tie—and a pair of run-down sneakers.

The church official shook my hand, and then I watched as his eyes lowered to the floor. My long hair was trouble enough. And now this.

"You know, Bill, that your reputation goes before you," he said.

"Yes, sir," I responded, not quite knowing what he meant.

Then he smiled and said, "We're not so concerned about what the man does. We are interested in what the man is."

I answered by saying, "What the man does is a direct reflection of what the man is."

When it comes to transferring knowledge, I can teach anybody the skills and techniques I know. But that does not mean the person is going to be able to perform in the same way I do, or that he will stick with the task.

What I have learned from experience is to first find a person with the right qualities, then begin to give them knowledge. Find someone who is investable. Then invest in them. For that reason I believe Sunday school teachers should constantly seek out young people who have the potential to be outstanding men and women of God. Then the teachers should spend time developing the skills and talents of those particular ones.

Mark Buntain, the great missionary, lived in the same apartment in downtown Calcutta for thirty-six years. In America some only knew of Buntain because of his reputation. In India they knew him for his character.

Years ago I read an interesting comparison between reputation and character.

> Reputation is what you are supposed to be.
> Character is what you are.
> Reputation is a photograph.
> Character is your face.

Reputation is what you have when you come to a new place.
Character is what you have when you go away.
Reputation is learned in an hour.
Character does not come to light for years.
Reputation is made in a moment.
Character is built in a lifetime.
Reputation grows like a mushroom.
Character grows like an oak.
Reputation is made from a single newspaper report.
Character is built from a life of toil.
Reputation makes you rich or poor.
Character makes you happy or miserable.
Reputation is what men say about you on your tombstone.
Character is what the angels say about you around the
throne of God.

Principle #4: *The "good" always has been and always will be the enemy of the "best."*

Scholastic test scores have been declining in America because students compare themselves with each other rather than chart their own personal improvement.

We live in a "good enough" society. If we make a C, that is good enough.

On the job people are more concerned with "getting by" and staying on the payroll than being productive in developing their personal growth. I have observed people who spend more time trying to escape work than it would take to go ahead and finish the task—especially in the ministry. It's ridiculous. A level of normalcy as far as work ethic has been established in ministry pretty much across the board. So all that's expected of young ministers coming into the ministry is fulfill your job description, go home, watch TV, and that's good enough. It's not enough!

Knowledge is like a pyramid. The closer you get to the top, the more you know about less and less. Finally you focus your attention on one single objective and decide that being good in that particular area is not enough. You make the determination to be the best.

As a representative of the King of kings, each one of us needs to make a commitment to excellence. Our objective should not be to maintain, to be like everyone else we see around us, but to grow.

It may be good to succeed in business or industry, but it is much better to succeed in life. It is good to attend church, but it is better to be known as a man or woman who knows the Lord.

As Christians we should not settle for what is average. Instead we should give God our best by obeying Scripture: "Whatever your hand finds to do, do it with all your might . . ." (Eccles. 9:10).

Principle #5: *You will only be remembered for two things in life: the problems you solve and the problems you create.*

I wish everyone reading this principle could get it into his or her head today. After twenty-five years of being around every sort of Christian ministry and minister—particularly the ones that I have worked with very closely—if someone mentions their name I can immediately put them, either consciously or subconsciously, in one of those two categories. I will immediately recall that they were a high-maintenance or a low-maintenance person. Their attitudes and actions will immediately be brought to my mind, and I can certainly remember if they were a joy to be around or whether they took so much of my time that I almost hated to see them coming. If you know what I mean.

All of us will be remembered by our co-workers in one of these two ways. The way that you will be remembered will be decided by you.

Principle #6: *What happens in you is more important than what happens to you.*

Several years ago I was in Dallas for a speaking engagement. The pastor picked me up at the airport and told me he had to make an emergency visit before he dropped me off at the hotel. A young couple in his church had just lost their year-old baby very suddenly.

Now a small child dying is bad enough, but it was only a few days before Christmas. We got to the house, and I'll never forget the whole scene. People crying, the dead child's presents still under the tree. The pastor did his best to console, but it was a tough situation at best.

I was back at that same church a few years later. I asked the pastor about the young couple. His response was interesting.

"After the funeral," he told me, "the woman decided to turn her grief into blessing. Every day she opens the obituary column of the *Dallas Times Herald*." Her pastor told me why she does this. "If she reads that a little child has died, she drives to the home of the family and comforts them. She understands and can say things that no one else can."

As a result of her ministry she has won a growing number of mothers to the Lord. She found recovery when she realized that what happens in you is far more important than what happens to you.

Instead of becoming bitter and turning her back on God, as many Christians I know have, she decided to be one who brings comfort and wipes away the tears. She said, "I'm going to turn this tragedy into triumph."

In the ghettos of New York, and now in other cities, we are presenting a message that transforms the young people on the inside—so that they will be able to resist the forces that try to destroy them daily.

Principle #7: *You cannot unscramble eggs.*

Once a mistake has been made you've got to move on. I could tell you story after story of senior pastors, staff members, right down to the secretaries who totally missed the will of God because they became victims of their own mistakes. People will criticize you when you make a mistake, and there are some people who are just waiting for you to do it so they can have something to criticize you for.

You need to understand that people are not your enemies. They are just a tool of our real enemy, Satan. Unfortunately, most of them are not even smart enough to know that they are being used as a tool of the enemy. When a mistake is made, acknowledge it, rectify it if possible, make apologies when necessary, find out why it happened, learn from it and move on.

The greatest asset I had as a young man growing up was my home pastor's giving me the right to fail. He believed in me, and he had faith and confidence in me; when I made mistakes, that trust and confidence never wavered. If it did, it was never displayed to me. In our staff here in New York I encourage people to step out, try new things, be creative. If it works, praise God—we all benefit. If it doesn't, then let's try something else. Babe Ruth was not only the home-run king; he was the strike-out king as well.

There is a little saying I use while trying to find new staff members who can survive here in New York. I always say, "You have to kiss a lot of frogs to find the prince." Now I have kissed a lot of frogs in my lifetime, but that little saying can also be applied to a lot of other facets of our ministry. If you're going to accomplish anything, you're going to make mistakes. If you quit for fear of failure, you'll be a quitter all your life.

Consider Abraham Lincoln's record.

> In 1831 he failed in business.
> In 1832 he was defeated for legislature.
> In 1833 he failed in business again.
> In 1834 he was elected to legislature, but in 1835 his sweetheart died.
> In 1836 he suffered a nervous breakdown.
> In 1838 he was defeated for speaker.
> In 1840 he was defeated for elector.
> In 1843 he was defeated for Congress.
> In 1846 he was elected to Congress, but in 1848 he was defeated for Congress again.
> In 1855 he was defeated for Senate.
> In 1856 he was defeated for vice president.
> In 1858 he was defeated for Senate.
> In 1860 he became president.

I think the life of Lincoln pretty much says it all. You can't undo defeats, and there are many wrongs that cannot be righted. But you can always keep going.

The road to accomplishment is filled with a lot of tempting parking places. Don't stop. Remember, even if you are on the right track, if you stop you are going to get run over.

Principle #8: *When you get something you never had, you become responsible for doing something you have never done.*

I am constantly amazed how so many people respond when they begin to progress in ministry. God blesses, new contacts are made, new methods are learned, new motivation is acquired. Nine times out of ten it seems that when things get moving, we become so caught up with the gift that we forget the Giver and the very reason the gift was bestowed upon us in the first place. We are nothing but a channel—the more income that comes our way, the more the outflow should rise proportionally.

The acquisition of added finances, staff, buildings, supporters or whatever is necessary for you to get the job done where you are should be looked at as nothing more than a green flag to say, "OK, to whom much is given, now much is required, and now I'm able to take these newly acquired tools and do more than what I have been able to do in the past."

Principle #9: *If people don't know your passion, you don't have any.*

In my travels I have been very observant of what pastors, staff members and generally people in the ministry talk about when they are not "on." Everything from their golf game to their vacation to their grandkids to where they buy their clothes. I say this sadly, but I feel as if I have to say it: Very seldom do any of these people speak about what they do in the ministry with a fervent passion. Very seldom do these things dominate the conversation. It seems easier to talk about something else—the normal mundane things in life rather than what they are involved in for God and the eternal things that they represent.

It doesn't take people very long when they come to visit New York to find out what our obsession is. And whenever they see us here or whenever they see us out of this city, there's an obvious passion for souls, a deep caring for children; there's a burden for the cities of this country; and there's an obsession that just can't be shaken off by casual conversation in an attempt to be socially acceptable. Bobby Sands, a former leader in the Irish Republican Army, starved himself to death for their political cause. There was a man several years ago out West who sat on a railroad track in protest of nuclear power and had several parts of his body severed because he believed in his cause so strongly.

We can look all of the way through history and see men and women who have been so consumed with their obsession that there was never a question in the mind of those around them what their life was being lived for and what their heart was committed to. Why can't we have Christians who are that passionate about what we believe today? I think we can, and I think we will.

Principle #10: *Being faithful is more important than being successful.*

In a small church in Scotland in the 1800s, the board of deacons came to their elderly pastor and said, "We feel that the time has come for you to step down as our pastor. Last year you had only one convert, a nine-year-old boy."

The boy's name was Robert. The pastor had taken the child into his home because the boy's family could no longer care for him. A strong bond developed between them. But now the elderly pastor had been dismissed from his church and was gone. And the old man and the young boy became separated.

But nearly twenty years later that boy became a great scholar and translated the Bible into several different languages. His name was Robert Moffat.

Robert Moffat grew into a man who would one day command the attention of kings and was known throughout the world as the father of foreign missions.

In an address at an English university, Moffat made a statement: "There is a land in the north of Africa that has never been reached with the gospel. I saw the smoke of a thousand villages that have never heard the gospel message."

Then he said, "Someone has to go."

There was a student in the audience in the second to the last row on the right-hand side. That young man said to himself, *I will be that man.*

The young man's name was David Livingstone.

For years nobody seemed interested in his work in the uncharted jungles of Africa. But slowly the story of his endeavors spread throughout Europe. When he died at Lake Banweulu in central Africa, the king of England sent for his body to be brought to London for burial in Westminster Abbey with royalty.

The Africans said, "No. He would want to be buried here. This is where he gave his life. His heart was here with us." But the king and Livingstone's denominational officials would not hear of it. It's funny. When he was alive, nobody cared if he lived or died. But once he was dead, everyone wanted to claim him.

The agents of the king persisted, and the ship set sail from London to get his body. But the night before his body was sent back to England, two of Livingstone's converts snuck into where his body was lying and cut out his heart. Today David Livingstone's body is buried in Westminster Abbey in England, but his heart is buried in Africa.

Years before, many believed the old minister in Scotland was a failure. They would never know what impact his devotion to one child would have on thousands of future missionaries and converts for years to come.

I've heard it said many years ago, "It's not as important what you accomplish in life as what you set into motion."

The ministry of Jesus lasted only three and a half years. But think of what is now being accomplished in His name because something was set into motion.

When you stand before the Lord, He will not ask if you were successful, but rather, "Were you faithful?"

I believe that Sunday school should be the most exciting hour of the week. It should attract the largest number of young people possible. But that is not what will open heaven's door—for me or for the young people we work so hard to reach.

Each of us must have a personal relationship with Christ. And it is only through the faithfulness of that preaching and setting the example that seeds will be sown that will never die.

It is my most fervent desire that one day all of us will hear Him say, "Well done, My good and faithful servant." We've got a lot of good starters in this thing, but not many finishers. After it's all over, how will you be remembered?

Left: Kids pass the time by showing off some street acrobatic skills.

Below: A little junkyard gymnastics using an old bedspring as a makeshift trampoline.

CHAPTER ELEVEN

From a Ministry to a Movement

I BELIEVE THAT GOD periodically and sovereignly raises up churches and ministries to do the obvious. And Metro is a pretty good example of doing the obvious because so much of what we do is based on taking care of the needs of the people—the need really is the call.

After several printings of this book, the need to update it became apparent. *Whose Child Is This?* has been in print for seven years, and during this period Metro has transitioned from a ministry to a movement. Even our corporate name has changed to Metro Ministries International to reflect the growing reality of what is taking place.

The number of children we are reaching in New York's inner city has doubled to well over twenty thousand kids each week. The demand for our conferences and training is backlogged. The people involved in children's ministry who have used our curriculum or read about the ministry want to learn more. They are duplicating what we do in New York, and it's making a difference in every type of city that you can imagine. They are stepping outside of the box in their own cities, and as they grow, they have a lot of questions. Of course, we've gained a lot of answers from our own school of hard knocks, so we're able to help them.

Ministries are pretty easy to track—but movements take on a

life of their own. It's very obvious when you look at what has happened with our concept of Sidewalk Sunday School. Metro has ignited so many other ministries to begin outreaches to kids that we can't even keep track of the hundreds of Sidewalk Sunday School ministries that have begun in cities all around the globe.

The curriculum that we write has more than quadrupled in the past seven years. It's marketed under the brand name of KIDS Church, and the whole thing has become so popular that KIDS Church has become synonymous with our way of doing Sunday school. Most recently the publisher, CharismaLife, has translated the Power Tool Box (the first year of KIDS Church) into Spanish—*Iglesia Para Niños.*

Why is the curriculum so popular? Is it some slick marketing campaign? No. The curriculum is popular and it sells because it's based on real lessons that have been taught—and today's ministries are looking for resources that really work. KIDS Church does that. This is happening in spite of all the people who said I couldn't write curriculum—but I do. And for the record, I can't write books either—but I do. I do because there is a need for this stuff.

Many new opportunities have emerged for Metro, and it's pretty amazing to stop and observe how this whole movement thing has mushroomed. The worldwide conferences in Europe, South America, Africa, Australia and Asia are happening all the time. From those conferences we've been overwhelmed with the number of international visitors who want to come to New York and learn firsthand how our ministry works. Once again we saw another need—a new international need was coming into focus, and the movement could not be contained in only New York City or North America.

We wanted to do something more for our international visitors, because if they could catch the vision of this thing, they could do a better job of training others in their own countries. About the same time that all this was busting loose, we had an opportunity to acquire a building that could be converted to a dormitory—a building that could house our international students. We got the building, stretched ourselves some more and created an on-site training center for people from other nations.

The international students come alongside of our team to learn it and live it. They do the hard work of the ministry just as we do, and they quickly gain an understanding of how they can make a difference. When these students go home, they are forever changed. Can you see the potential? One of the international conferences I spoke at said it this way, "Reaching kids—changing nations." I actually believe that's possible. And I am convinced that our on-site training facility is an integral part of the process.

It only takes one person to catch the vision, just as it did for a former missionary to Italy. This woman had basically lost hope in the work that she was so drawn to do; she really wanted to bring people to the Lord, but because of a multitude of problems, the missionary thing wasn't working. Fortunately, she showed up at a conference in England where I was speaking. Something connected for her that day, and she knew she had to do something.

So she came to New York. This woman was determined to learn what it is we do and how we do it. It didn't take a committee to help get her to New York—she just came on her own. By the time she returned to Naples, she was confident that she was going to make a difference—and she *is* making a difference. Her ministry is now reaching over nine hundred kids a week.

In Belfast, Ireland, we helped set up a Sidewalk Sunday School. What's interesting about this particular outreach is that it is conducted in the public school system. The weather in Belfast would cause a lot of challenges for our typical outdoor Sidewalk Sunday School program, so the opportunity to minister to the kids in public school is really unique—and the Belfast team is reaching one to two thousand kids a week.

Liverpool, England, has its own Metro Ministries operation. They are making a difference with Sidewalk Sunday School, and they do have a truck. The Liverpool office also serves as a catalyst for launching other European Metro branches, like the start-up in Amsterdam where we will be utilizing another Sidewalk Sunday School truck to reach kids in that city. We now have Metro branches in Holland, Germany and Switzerland.

The operation in Switzerland has given us a new vision for meeting the basic needs of people. It was a contact with one of the upper people in the Swiss military that showed us a mobile bakery that the Swiss had designed for field use. We linked the idea with our Sidewalk Sunday School trucks. We realized that a mobile bakery could be pulled by one of our trucks. And these mobile Swiss bakeries are amazing—they've come up with a system to turn out a thousand loaves of bread in a very short period of time. Can you see how this could help us reach families? We're already mapping out how we could move operations into Romania and places like Mongolia.

About the same time we established a full-time Spanish ministry in New York City, doors started opening up for us in South America. And now with *Iglesia Para Ninos* (the Spanish KIDS Church curriculum), we actually have resources to put into the hands of children's ministry leaders. The leaders of our New York Spanish congregation are setting up and speaking at the South American conferences and providing hands-on training. Many churches and individuals are catching the vision, and Sidewalk Sunday School operations are making a difference in those countries. One of our more unique ambitions is to build and equip a boat to travel down the Amazon River, conducting Sidewalk Sunday School on the river's banks.

In the last few years we've also made a lot of progress in some of the Asian countries. Our first efforts were in Singapore and Malaysia. We worked with a local ministry to do the seminars and train people. We demonstrated our time-tested principles of reaching kids, and it didn't take long for a lot of people to catch the vision of this thing. One of the men who caught the vision quit his corporate management position with McDonald's in Singapore. This man went into Cambodia using the materials from Power Tool Box (our first year of KIDS Church). He utilized our principles and resources to train the underground church in Cambodia. The window of opportunity was only open for a short time, and the man had to get back out—but the people in the underground church now have a vision of how to reach the kids.

A year after we were in Singapore, the KIDS Church program was going so strong in a local church, City Harvest Church, that they put on a demonstration for us. It's interesting to watch another culture doing what we do. The members of City Harvest Church started going door to door in the apartment complexes around their church to reach the kids. It didn't take them long to establish a thriving bus ministry. I think these folks might have the potential to move this thing into mainland China.

We've also ventured into the Philippines and its garbage dumps. The people who took me out to this awful site wanted me just to have a look and leave. But if you know anything about me, I'm not like that. For me to have a commitment to something I need to smell it and taste it first. Besides, you never reach anyone sitting on the sidelines.

So I walked down into the dump. I remember seeing a little boy who was about two years old. He was leaning up against one of the tiny shacks, surrounded by mounds and mounds of garbage. The boy was understandably sick, and feces were running from his little bottom. The poor kid didn't even have the strength to stand up. Nearby were two little girls. They were laughing and delighted to be grilling some chicken intestines they had found. Instead of a grill, though, they were preparing their meal over burning garbage. What do you say when you see something like this? What do you do?

For us it meant making an investment and a commitment to do something. Within months we had the opportunity to train leaders in the Philippines, hoping that someone would catch the vision. Thousands of people showed up, including some who came by boat and others who walked. One man did catch the vision. He comes from a well-to-do family and was educated in the United States. His father operates a factory in Manila for a major U.S. corporation. But this guy was willing to set all the comforts aside and reach kids for the Lord—something happened for this man. We worked with him to establish Metro Ministries Manila. And within a very short period of time, this man, in partnership with area churches, has taken the ministry to the streets and dumps of the Philippines, reaching over eight thousand kids. So, what do you think? Has this thing transitioned from a ministry into a movement? Either way, it all goes back to New York City for me.

Whose Child Is This?

I would like to tell you that when I first went to New York City I had it all figured out. It would be great to tell you that I had a five-year plan, a ten-year plan, an organizational structure chart and a budget. But I can't. I had no idea how to make the whole thing work, but I just knew I had to do something. For years I listened to so-called experts who said that what was on my heart couldn't be done in the inner city—especially New York City.

There was no way I could sit back and develop a plan or structure because I had no idea what it was that I was going to do. I wanted to do something, and anything had to be better than listening to all the people who said it wouldn't work. All that talk didn't jive with me. I thought, *"If the gospel doesn't work in the inner city, then it doesn't work—period."* If this gospel is not true in Calcutta, then it's not true in Honolulu. If it's not true in Brooklyn, then it's not true in Kansas City. The gospel is the gospel, and I was convinced that I could do something.

After speaking at one particular conference, I was spending time talking to people and answering their questions. I had a lot on my mind, because before coming to speak at the conference I conducted a funeral for a little six-year-old boy. He was not on my bus route, but he was one of the kids that our Metro team had reached out to. About a half-hour before the funeral, I went over to the funeral home. We use one local funeral home in particular, and knowing the layout of the place, I went looking for one of the directors. I went upstairs, and the woman who was working on the little boy's body said, "We don't have any clothes to bury this little boy in." I thought, *OK...we can take care of that.* We're constantly supplying used clothing for needy families. So, I ran back to the church and got a pair of pants, a little shirt and some shoes for the boy. I took the time to help the woman dress this little dead boy. I'm not going to describe how that feels—but it changes you.

As I helped dress the boy, I noticed gouges or dig marks of some kind on the side of his face and the back of his hand at the wrist. I turned to the woman and said, "You didn't do a very good job of covering this."

She replied, "You're not aware of what happened to him, are you?"

I said, "No, I'm not."

She continued, "The mother hit the kid with a baseball bat and busted his head open. Then she left her dead son lying on the floor all night. The house cats starting chewing on this kid's face and hands. That's why he's full of marks, and that's why nobody is coming to his funeral."

The little boy deserved a decent funeral. With or without anyone attending, I was determined to do something for this kid. We had the funeral and loaded his little casket into the hearse to take him to New Jersey. A burial plot had been arranged there. As we were putting the casket in the hearse, his grandmother came over to me and asked, "Can I talk to you for just a minute? I just wanted you to know that whenever my grandson came home from Sunday school, he would say, 'Grandma, I think those people at church love me. They always say that they love me, so I think that they really love me.' And he would always sing the songs you taught him. I wanted to come by to tell you thank you—because nobody ever really loved him. Thank you for loving him."

You can imagine how something like that sticks with you.

All that was on my mind during the pastor's conference at which I was speaking. After the conference, one of the ladies was trying to convince me that I didn't need to live in the ghetto. She said, "You've been beat up. You've been stabbed, and you've been through so much. I don't understand why you can't live someplace decent and commute. I just don't understand it."

How do you explain that to somebody? Well, you don't; you just don't. However, in this particular case someone spoke up for me. There was an old man nearby, and he was listening to our conversation. He walked up to the lady and stuck his finger in her face. "Lady, you will never understand what this man does because you don't have a shepherd's heart. You need to shut up and just leave him alone!" She looked a little shell-shocked, and then she turned around and left.

A shepherd's heart? The phrase stuck with me. What exactly does it mean to have a shepherd's heart? The whole thing caught my attention, and I decided to study the term. I got out a concordance and started flipping through all the references on sheep, lambs and shepherds. Almost everything I found I already knew, but it didn't click. But I did find one story that gave me an interesting illustration, and when I read it, it clicked!

I don't know if you will see it the way I saw it, but I want you to look at Amos 3:12. It's an interesting illustration of a lion, a lamb and the shepherd.

> As a shepherd takes from the mouth of a lion two legs or a piece of an ear...

In the illustration a lamb gets caught in the jaws of a lion, but it doesn't say why the lamb gets caught—it just says that it is caught. When I first read that I was able to visualize it. I realized that whenever a lamb gets caught...Or to put it another way, when someone gets into trouble, most of us are very concerned about whose fault it is. Am I right, or am I wrong? We're asking things like, Who did it? What happened? If a man is involved in a car wreck and is lying bleeding on the street, can you imagine a paramedic coming up to him and asking, "Whose fault is it? Were you drinking? Did you run the light?" Can you see how ridiculous that is? The paramedic's job is to do whatever it takes to save the man. Are you getting the picture?

The lamb is caught in the jaws of the lion. The shepherd comes up, and he has two choices. In this case, he just makes a move. I know what that feels like. It's an instinct; you know you've got to do something—anything—other than standing there and doing nothing. You don't have to think about it, because if you have a shepherd's heart, there is something in the heart that separates you from everybody else. There is a certain group—a minority group of people—that have a different kind of heart, a different kind of heart that responds when they see the need; they just move.

The shepherd runs over and tries to pull the lamb out of the jaws of the lion. He tries so hard to pull the lamb out of the lion's jaw that he ends up pulling off the lamb's leg. He's got a leg—it's hopeless. The easiest thing to do at this point is to just walk away, but he doesn't. The shepherd's heart is still crying. If you have a shepherd's heart, you cannot just walk away. The shepherd goes back a second time. What's the point? After all, the lamb is dying. But the shepherd goes back a second time and grabs another leg. He ends up pulling that leg off, too. Do you stop? The shepherd didn't. However, you know at some point the lion is going to attack the shepherd, and it will come down to personal sacrifice. Can you hang in there when it seems so hopeless? If you go back in, you might die—maybe. But the shepherd goes back a third time, even when it doesn't make any sense. In a last ditch effort, he reaches out and rips off a piece of the lamb's ear. Two legs and a piece of an ear—why?

Metro Ministries may have transitioned into a movement, but you'll still find me standing on Evergreen Avenue and Twelfth Street in Brooklyn, New York. The only thing I may be holding on to are two legs and a piece of an ear. But I think you know why.

The crowds of kids are a continual testimony to Sidewalk Sunday
School's popularity.

CHAPTER TWELVE

Can One Person Make a Difference?

I LEARNED A LONG time ago I can only speak from where I am in life. And when you've lived in the ghetto for as long as I have, it not only gives you a unique perspective, but it also changes your thinking. It's easy for us to pick up a newspaper and read about violence and then set the paper down. It's not so easy to set it down when you live where I live. You can't turn the page when you're standing in the street and witnessing the fights and the shootouts as I have. I've already seen twenty-one murders. When the violence is that close to your face, it changes your thinking. It causes you to think differently about what ministry is—and what it needs to be.

Where I am in life helps me see beyond the headlines and into the lives of the people on both sides of the violence, most of whom will never come into a church for whatever reason—some obvious reasons and some not so obvious. Although they may not be the kind of people we would go out of our way to try to be around, they are real people, and someone needs to reach them at some level—but can one man make a difference?

In the Book of Numbers, chapter 16, the children of Israel were, once again, complaining. They made a way of life out of that. Whatever God did, the children of Israel didn't like it. They didn't like the water. They didn't like the food. The children of Israel

161

didn't like the leadership or much of anything. The people were actually beyond complaining about Moses and Aaron—they were moving toward a revolution. The children of Israel were upset because Moses and Aaron were trying to get them to become more spiritual. The people didn't want it. They didn't want to change.

Moses and Aaron were attempting to help the children of Israel move closer to God, but the people really didn't want to do so. And it caused the people's rebellious attitude to grow. After all, everyone likes to do what he or she wants to do—no big revelations there. But the conflict escalated, and the children of Israel were positioning themselves to overthrow the leadership. Picture it: You have Moses and Aaron trying to lead the people closer to God, and a couple million Jews saying, "No way! We aren't going to change." Things aren't going good. It's not going well for Moses and Aaron.

It's at this point that God has His say. As I see it, God basically says, "Fine! You don't like the leadership. You don't like what I've given to you. No problem—I'm just going to kill all of you." And that's one of the things I like about God. Do you want to know why? God takes it. He takes it, and He continues to take it until finally one day He doesn't take it anymore.

Again, picture it with me. You've got Moses and Aaron and several million people. What happens next is really difficult to explain, but suddenly a wave of death starts to come across the crowd. People are falling over dead, and the body count is huge. If you choose to study this, you will find that fourteen thousand seven hundred people died in this plague. Do you know what's sad? For most people who read this account in the Book of Numbers, it's just a biblical statistic—just another one of those stories in the Bible. But don't let it be a statistic for you. Fourteen thousand seven hundred children of Israel fell over dead. They aren't getting up. And unless you have a point of reference, it's difficult for this to be anything more than a biblical statistic.

When it comes to death, I do have a point of reference. As I have already mentioned, I've witnessed twenty-one homicides in New York City—the place I've chosen to live. And when you're standing as close as I have to murder, watching the fire come out of the gun's barrel and the side of a man's head being blown off, it changes the way you think. That's what happens when you allow yourself to be around the urgency of life. The urgency changes you. It's why I still live in a warehouse in the ghetto. It is not because I have to—it's because I've *chosen to*. But can one man make a difference?

I was invited to speak at a Southern Baptist Bible conference in Florida. It's a very memorable conference for me because of what one of the pastors asked me after I spoke. This pastor challenged me with his question. He asked me, "Do you honestly think or believe in your gut that one person can make a difference in this thing we call Christianity? Or is this just something that people like you say to people like us to get us to do something?"

We all say that one person can make a difference—it's nice preacher talk; it makes a nice message. Proclaiming that one person can make a difference sounds good in Bible school, and it sounds good in a conference—it makes for happy Christian talk. But do we really believe it? That's what the preacher was asking me. I didn't give him a cute little answer. I answered him, "I don't know..." That's what I told him, and I took his question so seriously that I told him I wanted to think about it. "I'm going to answer your question, but I need time. It's so valid it deserves some time. But, I will answer you." His question led me to study what was going on with Moses and Aaron in Numbers 16.

The children of Israel were complaining. Whatever God did, the children of Israel didn't like it. They didn't like the water. They didn't like the food. The children of Israel didn't like the leadership. And now the people are falling over dead. It's at this point that the story takes an interesting twist. Moses turns to Aaron and yells, "Aaron, go do something!" Moses is telling Aaron to do something because they had never faced a situation like this—and what do you do when people are dropping over dead?

Recognize that Moses and Aaron were close enough to the action to be affected. The leaders were so close to what was happening that it demanded a response from them. Moses told Aaron to do something. "Run to the altar; go do something!" The urgency is screaming—it demands action. The urgency moved

Aaron to run and grab a censer. If you're familiar with the furnishing of the tabernacle, the censer is the stick-like thing with a cup on it. Aaron grabs the censer and runs to the altar. He uses the censer to scoop up some fire from the altar. Next, Aaron runs into the middle of the crowd, carrying the censer, but I'm convinced he doesn't really know what he is going to do. Aaron was obeying Moses' command to do something. Here is what the Bible says:

> And he stood between the dead and the living; so the plague
> was stopped.
>
> —NUMBERS 16:48

The forty-eighth verse says it all. Aaron stood between the living and the dead. Where he stood, the dying stopped. Are you with me?

The question the Baptist pastor asked me was, "Do you honestly believe that one person can make a difference?" What do you think? In the above account, even the casual reader would have to agree that Aaron made a difference. One man made a difference, but what did he have to do? Aaron had to run to the altar, get some fire and then he had to go into the crowd. He just went—didn't he?

So, if one person can make a difference, and it's obvious just in this one segment that one person can make a difference, what kind of person can make a difference?

Let's take a closer look at Aaron. As I began to study this account, I noticed that Aaron and the fire was all that stood between the living and the dead. It was just Aaron and the fire. It wasn't something the denomination came up with. There wasn't a congregation involved—not even a committee. One man made the move. And this isn't the only biblical account of one man or one woman making a difference. In those situations, something happened to the individual, and that individual became the catalyst for all that followed—they made a difference.

In our ministry, we visit every kid every week—and that means making over twenty thousand personal visits. It's difficult to write about it because it sounds as if you're lying. People do ask, "How in the world can you visit twenty thousand kids every week?" We just do. And what we do is very physical ministry—it takes a lot of physical labor to do the visits, the Sidewalk Sunday School, the bus ministry, the camps, Holiday Hope and the support work to keep this thing running. But we just do it, and we keep doing it.

More importantly, we build relationships. We don't just knock on the doors; we build relationships with the people. We've got a lot of hard workers making a difference. Workers like the two young ladies who handled the visitation for one of our Sidewalk Sunday School sites in the Morris Housing Project in the South Bronx. It's a really tough area, but they just did it.

One of the families on their route included a seven-year-old girl and her younger brother who was five or six years old. The children were not mentally retarded, but they were just slow. They were good kids who faithfully showed up for Sidewalk Sunday School. They were there every week.

However, one week the kids missed, and our workers were understandably concerned. A few days later the young women went to visit the children to make sure they were OK and invite them to the next Sidewalk Sunday School service. They went to the door and knocked. They kept knocking, but no one came to answer the door. It was odd, because the workers could hear the television—it was on, but nobody would answer the door.

Our workers had a relationship with this family, and because of the condition of the kids the mother was always home. The girls went next door, thinking that the neighbors would know what was going on—but the neighbors couldn't help or answer any of their questions. So, our workers went back and again began to beat on the door—but no one answered. However, this time the young women noticed a strange smell coming from the apartment. When no one in the building could help our workers, they called the police.

Every police precinct in New York City has a special unit called the ESU—Emergency Service Unit, and that's what the police in the South Bronx dispatched for the call. The officer in charge of the ESU determined that a break-in was warranted. Maybe you've seen the six-foot steel battering rams that cops use to break down doors. That's what they had to use to get into the apartment, as our workers waited to see if the kids were OK.

When the cops knocked down the door, the mother was lying on the living room floor. Her throat had been slit, and she had been dead for a week—which was causing the awful smell. The kids were in the living room, too. The girl and her younger brother were sitting on the couch watching television. They had eaten all the food in the apartment.

When our workers went in, they sat on the couch with the kids. The seven-year-old girl was holding a cereal box and was ripping the cardboard box into little pieces. The kids were eating the box—it was all they had.

About two weeks after the horrible discovery, one of the detectives from the precinct called me. He explained that their investigation did not turn up any fingerprints or leads. He was certain that they would never find out who had murdered the children's mother. Then he said, "That's not why I am calling you." He went on to explain that he had been a detective in the precinct for eighteen years, and then he added, "I talked to one of my officers who answered the call. He explained that after the ESU knocked down the door, they allowed your ministry workers to enter. He told me they stepped over the dead mother and sat on the couch with the children. Your workers put their arms around the kids and held them. They took care of them. In all my years of service, I've never seen that happen. To be honest with you, I've seen your Metro Ministry buses and trucks around the Bronx and never really paid much attention to your organization." The detective continued, "I still don't know exactly what you do, but on behalf of the New York City Police Department, whatever it is you are doing, I want to encourage you to keep doing it—because it looks like it's making a difference."

I was not there that day. The only ones making a difference were the two young women who, like Aaron, did something. They were visiting kids in the South Bronx that no one else cared about. But you won't see our young workers on the cover of a magazine. No one will be asking them to be guests on a television program. The Metro workers are not magazine material, and no one is asking them to be on TV. In fact, one of the workers in this story has a speech impediment, and the other one is very poor. But that day those two workers literally stood between the living and the dead—didn't they? They stood between the living and the dead, and they made a difference. Everyday people—regular workers. No hotshots or conference headliners—just regular ministry workers. Just faithful people who really care.

When I studied further about Aaron, I came across something that didn't make sense. Do you know how old Aaron was when all of this happened? Aaron was one hundred years old. What did Moses say? Run to the altar? A man who is one hundred years old running to the altar? It's impossible. You can't do it, Aaron. Your time has come and gone. It's impossible. But guess what? He did it.

Isn't it amazing what you can do—that you can't do? You hear it all the time. "Oh, I can't do that." Yes, you can—you just don't want to.

People don't expect me to drive a bus and pick up kids after all these years, but I do. "You shouldn't be doing that," they say. "You're the senior pastor. You can't drive the bus, too." I know that. But I am going to go and do it again next week. I'll keep driving the bus. Do you want to know how I can do that? I ran to an altar once and got some fire. I just went. It wasn't that big of a deal. I've been doing the same thing for over thirty years, and I think it's making a difference.

Think about how my mother left me on the culvert and never came back for me. Think about how one man, a Christian man, stopped and picked me up. He got me some food. That very day he paid my way to a youth camp, and I got saved. Can one person make a difference? Someone did for me.

A woman who couldn't speak English was saved in one of our adult services. After church she came to me and said through an interpreter, "I want to do something for God." I didn't really know what to tell her. I knew the language barrier would be a problem for the Puerto Rican woman because our workers must be able to communicate with everyone. So I told her just to love the kids. I explained, "We've got lots of buses. Just ride a different bus every week and love the kids. Well, she took my suggestion, and she just did it.

The woman didn't tell us that the week before she started riding the bus she got someone to teach her how to say "I love you" and "Jesus loves you" in English. That's all she could say. So she would ride a bus, sit in the front row and find the worst-looking kid in the bunch. She would take that kid and put him or her on her knee and whisper "I love you" and "Jesus loves you" all the way to Sunday school and back home again. That's all she could say—it was all she could do. But like Aaron, when someone told her to go do something, she did. In her own simple way she loved on the kids, and the process continued week after week. Early in the fall she told the bus ministry leaders that she didn't want to change buses any more. She had found one particular bus that she wanted to continue riding. Actually, there was one little boy on that bus that the Puerto Rican woman wanted to attend to—she wanted to focus her time on this one kid.

The little boy was about three years old. He was thin and always dirty. Even more significant was the fact that this kid never spoke a word. Somehow one of our workers reached out to this kid. They told him about Sunday school and how to catch the bus. And he came. Brothers and sisters or a neighborhood friend didn't join this little kid—he just rode the bus by himself. Every Saturday he would sit on the stairs in front of his apartment building waiting for the Metro Sunday school bus to pick him up.

And each time he boarded the bus the Puerto Rican lady was there waiting to greet him. She would take the little guy in her arms and put him on her lap. Then this woman would tell the boy again and again, "I love you" and "Jesus loves you." She would tell him that all the way to Sunday school. And she would repeat the same process on the ride back home. Week after week this same routine was repeated. That's all she could do—but she did it faithfully.

The weeks turned into months, and the routine never changed. The Puerto Rican woman loved on one little kid, letting him know, "I love you" and "Jesus loves you." About two weeks before Christmas, the routine did change. Like all the times before, the boy boarded the bus and received the love and attention of one woman who wanted to do something for God.

Together, they went to our Sunday school. And after Sunday school they boarded the bus for the ride home. On the ride home the woman took the young boy in her arms and put him on her lap. "I love you," she told him. "Jesus loves you." When the bus pulled to a stop in front of his apartment building, the boy didn't run off the bus as he normally did. This time as he started to leave, he turned around—and for the first time in our presence, this kid tried to speak. He looked at the Puerto Rican woman who wanted to do something for God and said, "Aah...aah...I...la-la-la...love...yoooou...ta...ta...too." And with that, the little boy put his arms around the woman who cared for him and gave her a big hug. That was 2:30 on a Saturday afternoon.

That very same evening, around 6:30, the little boy's dead body was discovered under the fire escape of his apartment building. On the same afternoon that one of our workers experienced a breakthrough in the life of that little kid, his own mother murdered him. She beat her son to death, put him in a garbage bag and threw him away.

Nobody in this thing called Christianity is qualified—but we all have a part to play, don't we? I am not the smartest guy, and I don't pretend to be. I am not a hotshot author or a ministry expert either. But I can drive a bus. And because others have come to join with me, I believe we are making a difference.

I believe today that there is one little boy in heaven because of a woman who couldn't speak English, but who had a burning desire to do something for God. I believe that one woman who took the time to hold a dirty little kid in her arms and tell him that she loved him and Jesus loved him made an eternal difference in the boy's life. No one who can convince me otherwise.

The Baptist pastor asked me, "Do you think one person can make a difference?"

Yeah, I do think one person can make a difference. What do you think? When it's all said and done, it's important for you and I to remember that out there—somewhere, today, right now—there's another kid who isn't making it. There is another kid sitting on a curb today. And all it takes is one person to make a difference in that kid's life.

Above: Bill Wilson and Senator John Ashcroft of Missouri survey the neighborhood surrounding Metro Ministries. President George Bush appointed both men to serve on the National Commission on America's Urban Families, which held one of its meetings at Metro.

Right: Elaborate grafitti memorials like this one are errected to commemorate where loved ones were killed.

CHAPTER THIRTEEN

This Child Is Mine

W HAT ARE THESE children going to become?" I have been asked that question hundreds of times. To me, it is the wrong question. I have said for years that I'm not nearly as interested in what these kids become as I am in what they don't become.

A weekend observer has a difficult time understanding that statement and what we really do here. They see an exciting program and a dedicated staff, but they fail to comprehend the depth of the challenge we face. Touching the lives of twenty thousand may sound impressive if you live in a community of forty thousand. But there are more than one million children in the five burroughs of New York. We are reaching less than 1 percent of them.

When I look at a street corner and see young adults involved in drugs, prostitution and everything in between, I think, "We could have reached them if we were here when they were younger."

Do I expect the children who now ride our buses to become doctors, lawyers and accountants? That may happen to one or two of these youngsters. But, again, I am not as concerned about their occupation as I am with keeping them out of the gutter. Success to me is that they are not on Flushing Avenue with the

171

hookers—or down on Troutman selling crack.

That is why we work as hard at this as we do.

I was thrilled when I recently talked with one of our former Yogi Bear Sunday school kids who is now a garbage collector. His starting salary was more than thirty-two thousand dollars a year. Compared with the alternative, his is an enormous achievement.

"I'm Staying Here"

OUR GOAL IS not to see our students finish high school or college and then move to a better community. That kind of thinking created the ghetto in the first place. Who is going to stay and fight the battle? Who is going to buy a house in Bushwick and be a catalyst for change?

One of our staff members encouraged a young lady with great potential to apply for a scholarship at a Christian college in Florida. The girl told her, "No way. Do you think I'm going to go off and leave my little sister in a place like this?"

What has happened to the young people in whom we have invested our lives? Some are in college. Some have stayed in the area and found employment. Some are preparing for full-time ministry. Some are now staff members at Metro.

I'm often asked, "Bill, will you ever have an 80, 90 or 100 percent success rate?"

Probably not.

Sociologists are examining the problem of the urban ghetto constantly. I tell them that only one out of every four young people here is going to make it in life. The parable of the seed and the four kinds of ground makes a lot of sense here, and it is very accurate. Ten years from today, if just half of those we are training become productive citizens and Christian parents, we will have doubled the success rate.

Deep in my heart I know that if what we are doing is not duplicated on a massive scale, we will fail millions of young people. That's why we are working so hard to see our curriculum placed in the hands of Christian educators and youth workers. What we present on Saturday mornings is incorporated into the programs published by CharismaLife and is now taught across the nation and overseas.

No Accountability

I WAS IN Los Angeles toward the end of the riots of 1992.

What happened there was not about Rodney King being beaten by the police. It was about a community filled with people who have no values—who have no relationship with Christ, which produces no accountability.

While in Los Angeles I had a conversation with a U.S. Army private whose unit was called in to help restore order. "The thing that troubled me the most," he said, "was the mother and two children who were running out of a store with their arms filled with merchandise."

Then he told me, "I rushed up to one of the boys and told him to put the merchandise back. The child was about eight or nine. He looked at me, a man in uniform, and said, 'I don't have to listen to you,' and then he followed his mother."

I don't claim to know every reason why our inner cities have failed. But as Christians we must revise our priorities regarding how we think about missions.

More than 90 percent of the world's foreign missions money comes from the United States. Supporting a Christian worker in Haiti or Hungary is good, but if we lose our own nation, we won't have to worry about sending any money anywhere anymore.

We need a massive invasion of Christian workers in our inner cities. For example, to effectively reach the children of an eight- or ten-square-block area requires one full-time worker. We need hundreds of staff members in New York City. This amount of people would be needed to conduct a similar ministry in any major city in America.

The Sidewalks of the World

DURING THE PAST several years we have developed a concept for reaching young people that is unlimited in its potential. It is the Sidewalk Sunday School.

Whose Child Is This?

The idea was implemented because Metro Church could not physically hold all of the children who needed to be reached. In reality it is a greatly improved version of the Neighborhood Bible Clubs I began in St. Petersburg many years ago.

Every day after school we go out to the neighborhoods where it is impractical for us to bus children to Sunday school. We have teams that take the trucks out to these different neighborhoods and conduct a Sunday school class outside in the parks or projects. The small trucks are customized to convert quickly into open-air stages. We go back to the same place at the same time every week. We stress the importance of visitation and they come, in all kinds of weather, not just the kids but the parents and the teens as well.

Everybody says that the church is not the building but the people, so we said, "OK, let's do it that way." We have actually formed a congregation with attendances that average anywhere between 150 to 500. It resembles a typical church congregation in many ways, from the opening prayer to the altar call. The only difference is that they meet outside.

Nearly fifty Sidewalk Sunday Schools are presented each week in the most needy areas of our city—the Lower East Side, Harlem and the South Bronx. One location is next to a shelter for homeless families.

Those on the front line of this program become more excited about it every week. A former staff member who directed the Lower East Side program told me, "If money were no object and you had dedicated people, this would probably be the number one ministry in the world. It is the most visible presentation of the gospel I've ever seen."

Some observers believe the concept is so powerful that it will be the spearhead of a modern-day revival. It is inexpensive to operate and is applicable to every town and city in America regardless of size or economic strata. It can be presented in lower, middle- and upper-middle-class neighborhoods.

We like to say, "The message is so simple that even adults can understand it."

The concept has been duplicated in over three hundred cities in the United States and in many parts of the world. We believe it is a movement that will touch millions worldwide.

No Excuses

YOU MAY SAY, "I'd love to become involved in something like this, but I just don't have the time."

I used to buy that excuse when I was nineteen. But I have learned that you make time in life for exactly what you want.

Do I have time to help start Sunday schools in other cities? In foreign countries? No. But I do it because it's important. We recently returned from training workers in Argentina where thousands of children attend what they call La Escuela en la Calle, or the "School on the Street"—their version of Sidewalk Sunday School. The flight was seventeen hours to get there and seventeen hours to get back. It was draining, but we make time for what we believe to be important.

Scripture tells us that to whom much is given, much is required. (See Luke 12:48.) I fully realize that someone rescued me as a boy who had no one. Now I have the joy of reaching out to young people in need.

"We Don't Want Him Anymore"

THOSE WERE THE words of a distraught couple who were standing at my door one night when I was a youth pastor in Florida. Their son Jason was with them.

"If you'll take him, he is yours," the father said.

Jason was the kind of kid who made instant enemies. He was a constant troublemaker—at school, at home and in the church.

The deacons in the church could be counted on to lose their tempers when he was around. One day Jason borrowed a motorcycle and rode it across the grass of the church just before a service. One of the deacons grabbed Jason by the shirt, lifted him up from the motorcycle and threw him to the ground. What happened next was not what you would expect from a deacon. He gave him a verbal chewing out that you'd imagine in a back-alley brawl. What a testimony!

Whose Child Is This?

People are not going to listen to you if they don't like you. Many people attend a church because they like the pastor or someone in the church. If they didn't, they wouldn't be there. That's the way it is.

I ran over to the scene of the motorcycle incident and tried to plead Jason's case with the deacon.

That night, at my apartment, I stood up for him again. I welcomed him into my home and raised him for the next few years as if he were my own flesh and blood.

His parents threw him away. But that is something Jesus would never do.

I've committed my life to repaying a debt I owe, not just to someone who lifted me up when I was down, but to Christ for giving His life for me at Calvary

The Strategy

THERE ARE CHILDREN in crisis in every city and every small town in America. Conflicts in the home are equally present in Manhattan, Kansas, and in Manhattan, New York. No matter where they live, underneath their façades people are identical. We only have *more* of them in New York. That's the only difference.

When nearly nine million people are jammed into an area of fifteen by thirty miles, it's no wonder we see such hostility and violence.

In counseling with youth directors and clergy nationwide, I have found that we all are dealing with the same human hassles and problems. Sin is sin, regardless of the location.

If we are going to see our nation turn to the Lord, our strategy should not be to try to win a city or a neighborhood or even a block. We have to come to the point where we are willing to win the nation one person at a time.

The success of our ministry is not the giant rally. It is individual people serving the Lord.

Television cameras and stadiums filled with people may have their place, but they will never equal the impact of a committed Christian living out the Christian life, serving in a local church, taking time to minister to a child who has lost his or her way.

We should never lose sight of the fact that God ordained the local church. It has greater value than any high-profile ministry you can name. That was the New Testament plan and still is. The local church has the potential for the leadership, discipleship and relationship necessary to fulfill God's mission.

You may say, "My church is dead! How can we turn it around?"

First of all, don't ever criticize your pastor. You don't always see what he sees. You are not carrying that load. Besides, it only takes one individual in a local congregation to revolutionize a church. I've seen it happen again and again. If the Lord is dealing with you to be that person, step forward and begin. We know the methods that work, and we can teach you how it is done. What we can't teach is a burden that burns within your soul—and a passion to win your city one person at a time. That is between you and God.

There will come a day when you say, "I don't care whether anybody joins me. I'm going full steam ahead to take this city one soul at a time for Christ." The moment you launch your effort, you will be surprised at how many people have been waiting for your leadership. The multiplication factor can produce a ministry beyond anything you have ever dreamed.

Today inner-city Sunday schools are springing up like giant mushrooms nationwide. Target locations, however, should not only be centers of poverty and crime. I believe the time is here to take a solid, upright, moral community and make the commitment to keep it that way. Great ministries don't need to be focused on intervention after drugs and perversion have taken their toll. They can be aimed at prevention so that young people will never have to experience the ravages of sin. We need to learn to pray, "Lord, help me reach them before their bodies and souls are soiled by Satan."

In many Third World nations 60 percent of the population is less than fourteen years old. Yet few missions organizations have a strategy to reach children. They'd rather have a tent crusade for adults or build a Bible school.

I've been in Mexico City and have seen the Friday and Saturday night street dances sponsored by the local Communist Party, where afterward Marxist political literature is passed out. Young people flock to the scene by the thousands. Why are we so slow to pick up on these concepts?

Bold Steps

ONCE A CRITIC of our program said, "Bill, you're brainwashing those kids!"

I wish that were possible. We only have them for one hour and a half each week. That is hardly a balance for the garbage that surrounds them every day of their lives.

If we are going to see lives change, we need to take unusual steps. The days of the funny little flannelboard stories in the Sunday school are over. Your presentation had better come from deep within your spirit and be presented with power and punch as if this were the last time the child will ever hear the gospel. We are fighting to reclaim our nation and the hearts of the youth.

Over the years I have seen a lot of good starters. But I have not seen many good finishers. There is only one way to finish the race, and that is to act boldly on your commitment. This is not a game we are playing. It is a matter of life and death. Every day it's life and death.

We will not win them all, but we will win one, and another, and another. On my bus route I talked recently with a young lady who has been coming to Metro Sunday school for years. She told me, "Pastor Bill, I just wanted you to know that half of everything I know in life I've learned from you."

We talked about it for a while and came to the conclusion that the values she learned were the result of our constant hammering away at basic themes. Week after week, we just keep hammering.

One of our bus workers, Millie, has been involved in our program since she was a teen. She is also the mother of two boys in our Sunday school. I asked her why she is still involved.

"I saw so many of my friends throwing their lives away," said Millie, "but the Sunday school changed my life."

Then she added, "I want my sons to become what I am now, a Christian."

Millie's husband is in federal prison. He was found guilty of murder.

"He picked the wrong friends," she explained. "I pray my boys will follow the path of Jesus."

We're Just Beginning

ARE WE SUCCESSFUL? Numbers are really only a by-product. The only measure worth talking about is what happens in the life of one child. But others experience benefits as well, including the community.

Before David Feingold, a Brooklyn director for government urban renewal, passed away, he told me, "One of the reasons Bushwick has been targeted for new, low-rent government housing is because of the difference your ministry has made in the feel and the attitude of the community. Because your ministry came, the area now looks 'investable.'"

Even to the secular society the transformation is obvious. But there's such a long road ahead.

On the platform of Metro Church, Norman Vincent Peale leaned over and said something I will never forget. The ninety-three-year-old positive thinker was there to present the *Guideposts* magazine Church of the Year award. He said, "You've accomplished a mighty work for God here, Son, but you've got a lot of years to go."

What about tomorrow? Do we still have dreams and plans?

Certainly! We need more housing for our workers, several larger buildings that will accommodate growth, more Sidewalk Sunday School trucks and more committed staff.

To date we've only touched about 5 percent of the city. In our first year we wanted to come in and put a Band-Aid on everything in sight—the hookers, the homeless, the drug addicts, the muggers.

Then we looked up and cried, "Lord, we can't meet all of these needs!"

Finally we learned to focus on the one thing that we do best. In my case, it is to influence the lives of children one at a time.

What are our limitations? In a nutshell they are workers and dollars. With dedicated people and financial support I know what can be done. I only pray that it will somehow happen faster. The program has inspired people from all over the country to begin new outreaches.

- Jim Davidson, a clinical psychologist from Ashtabula, Ohio, closed his practice and started the Heart and Hand ministry in Cleveland that has touched thousands.

- Bill Gray, a banker, took early retirement to start a large-scale children's ministry in Mobile, Alabama.

Our own program is now growing like a giant tree with branch Sunday Schools in Washington, D.C., Dallas/Ft. Worth, Houston, Detroit and Los Angeles.

I Had No Idea

DAVE RUDENIS, THE God-sent man who found me sitting on the culvert and paid my way to youth camp, was at a *This Is Your Life* program they surprised me with in Florida. "Did you think it would ever come to this?" I asked him.

He looked at me and said, "I had no idea." Then he added, "If I had the chance to do it over again, I'd do it the same way."

Dave has never received much recognition in his life. He's never been on television or addressed large crowds. He owns a machine shop, races cars and quietly serves the Lord in a local church. By most people's standards, he is just an average fellow.

But he saw a sad little boy and wondered, *Whose child is this?*

That day I became the call of God for him.

Dave's life may seem to be average, but just think of what he set in motion. I don't even want to think what my life would have become if Dave had not seen the need.

Every Saturday when I get behind the wheel of a big yellow bus, I know who my passengers will be.

Whose child is this?

This child is mine.

For a resource catalog or more information concerning Metro Ministries, please contact:

Metro Ministries International
P. O. Box 370695
Brooklyn, NY 11237-0695

(800) 462-7770

You can
experience more
of
God's grace
& love!

If you would like free information on how you can know God more deeply and experience His grace, love and power more fully in your life, simply write or e-mail us. We'll be delighted to send you information that will be a blessing to you.

To check out other titles from **Creation House** that will impact your life, be sure to visit your local Christian bookstore, or call this toll-free number:

1-800-599-5750

For free information from
Creation House:

CREATION HOUSE
600 Rinehart Rd.
Lake Mary, FL 32746
www.creationhouse.com